HOW THE WORLD RUNS

WORKBOOK

Kevin Swanson

Generations
PASSING ON THE FAITH

Printed in the United States of America
4th Printing, 2025

ISBN: 978-1-954745-40-7

Cover Design: Justin Turley
Interior Layout Design: Rei Suzuki Design, Ltd.
Published by:
Generations
PO Box 1398
Elizabeth, CO 80107
www.generations.org

For more information on this and
other titles from Generations,
visit www.generations.org or call 888-389-9080.

CONTENTS

COURSE INTRODUCTION

This course is geared for a high school student and should be treated as a core subject in the field of social science. Economics both in the macro and micro form is a basic preparatory course for life. Thus, this course should be treated as a 1 credit, full-year course, geared for the 14- to 18-year-old student.

In How the World Runs (And Your Part in It), Generations introduces a biblical world and life view to the field of economics. Using simple language, down-to-earth examples, and helpful allegorical explanations, the course helps students understand complex economic ideas in simple terms. Efforts have been made to explain difficult concepts at a 14-year-old level without losing the substance of the conceptual meaning. It was our goal that not a paragraph be uninteresting, vague, or too difficult. The approach taken maximizes on life integration, crossing over from macro-economics to micro-economics (for the individual and the family) throughout.

Basic math skills (including fractions, percentages, multiplication, and division) are a pre-requisite for the course. Simple statistics like averages and standard deviations are introduced. However, the text avoids use of algebraic equations.

The text includes hundreds of relevant biblical passages included in the text, so as to be sure that the Word of God is a "frontlet" or a "sign" set before the learner at all times (Deut. 6:8-9).

THE BIG PROJECT

This course requires work, not just schoolwork, but real work. To finish this course, the student will have to work. That may involve an entrepreneurial-business venture, a family economic project, or working for somebody else. If it is an entrepreneurial endeavor, the student will have to create a service or a product and sell it customer(s). If the work project involves laboring for somebody else, the student must still be involved at providing a product or service for customers. The work may or may not involve compensation or profit. That means the worker may not be paid for the work but may only profit by the experience. The work may be a construction project, a ministry project, lawn maintenance, a lemonade stand, writing a children's book for distribution, or a thousand other possibilities.

The Big Project should involve at least 72 hours of actual work at a minimum, over a period of 9 months, or 8 hours per month, or 2 hours per week. As a recommendation (not a requirement), the student should work on the project for 5 hours per week.

Assignments relating to "the Big Project" are contained at the back of this study guide. However, the project may be started up at any point. All of this should be conducted under the supervision of the parent or teacher assigned to the course.

A LITTLE MENTORSHIP

The second unique characteristic of this course is that it will require a mentor that can help the student with the big project. This is simply someone who is experienced in the field who can answer questions and provide guidance concerning the work. All of this should be conducted under the supervision of the parent or teacher assigned to the course.

THIS STUDENT WORKBOOK INCLUDES:

1. Lesson Schedule
2. Vocabulary Exercises
3. Study Questions
4. Life Integration and Spiritual Application
5. Final Exam
6. The Big Project
7. Glossary
8. Answer Key

COURSE OBJECTIVES

This course is dedicated to the glory of God and to the preeminence of the Lord Jesus Christ in all things. The essential objectives for the course must therefore be:

1. That our young men and women would begin to recognize the general calling God has on their lives.
2. That our young men and women would begin to recognize their talents and see the need to steward these talents.
3. That the students would see the sharp contrast between the world's hierarchy of values and priorities and God's values and priorities.
4. That the students would be able to apply God's law in the marketplace and wherever economic matters are involved.
5. That the students would be increasingly prepared to be good stewards, effective workers and producers, and thoughtful purchasers.
6. That the character of each student be better honed, that their identity as belonging to Christ be further established, and that they embrace God's purpose for their lives.
7. That the students be well equipped to understand economic markets, the workplace, entrepreneurism, how to get a job, how to be a good employee, how to communicate effectively in business, how to improve work performance, and what is a quality product or service.
8. That the students would be able to define success, and the things that contribute to success (or failure) in the workplace and the economy.
9. That the students would recognize the reasons for the failure of macro-economies in this generation.
10. That the students will learn by doing and begin to life integrate the knowledge they obtain in God's world of economy.
11. That our young men and women would know Scripture better and see its amazing relevance to every part of life (including economics), especially as the passages are meditated upon throughout the course.
12. That our students would learn to be more grateful and more ready to give God the praise and the glory for His goodness to us.

TEACHING METHOD

In order for this course to have maximum effect, the teacher/parent should:

1. Realize the joy and excitement of exploring God's world, God's principles relating to money and economy, and the blessing He provides us.
2. Love God.
3. Accept the obligation to follow through on knowledge by real life application. This curriculum and lesson schedule is laid out in a carefully designed manner, such that the lesson culminates in thanksgiving to God and practical life application.

The following presents the order of the learning process:

1. Read the material.
2. Work on the Big Project.
3. Complete the written lessons.
4. Work on the Big Project.
5. Finish the Final Exam at the End.

The parent/teacher may consider reading the material out loud. The text is designed to be engaging to all of our tween and teen children (ages 10-18), as well as parents and teachers.

LESSON SCHEDULE

The lesson schedule is provided as a suggestion—teachers/parents and students may adapt the schedule to suit their needs. The lesson schedule is based on a 36-week school year divided into two semesters. The schedule involves 3 days per week reading the text and completing the workbook exercises, and 2 days working "The Big Project." Of course, there may be flexibility as to how this ratio works out in a given week, or throughout the year. In other words, the book work will have to work around the student's work schedule.

GRADING

The Teacher/Parent may determine for themselves how they would grade the assignments. The following is recommended:

The Workbook Exercises are best suited for grading or at least checking for completion.

It is recommended that "The Big Project" be graded on the basis of the evaluations filled out by the mentor.

FINAL COURSE GRADE VALUES

To calculate the final course grade the parent/teacher may use the following recommended weighted score:

The Big Project - 40%
Completion of Study questions - 50%
Final Exam - 10%

Final Grade = 0.40 x (score for The Big Project) + 0.50 x (Degree to which Lessons were Completed Satisfactorily) + 0.10 x (final exam score)

90 to 100 percent = A
80-89 percent = B
70 to 79 percent = C
60 to 69 percent = D
0 to 59 percent = F

Our prayer is that this course be a blessing for thousands of young students who will serve the Lord, seek His kingdom first, and bless others—their future families, church communities, and the world at large.

> And God is able to make all grace abound toward you, that you, always having all sufficiency in all things, may have an abundance for every good work. As it is written: "He has dispersed abroad, He has given to the poor; His righteousness endures forever." Now may He who supplies seed to the sower, and bread for food, supply and multiply the seed you have sown and increase the fruits of your righteousness, while you are enriched in everything for all liberality, which causes thanksgiving through us to God. (2 Corinthians 9:8-11)

The Generations Curriculum Team
March, AD 2022

FIRST SEMESTER SUGGESTED DAILY SCHEDULE

Note: The Big Project is assigned for two days a week. This may occur on any two days (Monday through Saturday).

Date	Day	Assignment	Due Date	√	Grade
		First Semester-First Quarter			
Week 1	Day 1	Read Introduction			
	Day 2	Begin Reading Chapter 1			
	Day 3	Finish Reading Chapter 1			
	Day 4	The Big Project			
	Day 5	The Big Project			
Week 2	Day 1	Complete Chapter 1 Vocabulary Terms and Study Questions			
	Day 2	Begin Chapter 1 Life Integration and Spiritual Application			
	Day 3	Finish Chapter 1 Life-Integration and Spiritual Application			
	Day 4	The Big Project			
	Day 5	The Big Project			
Week 3	Day 1	Begin Reading Chapter 2			
	Day 2	Continue Reading Chapter 2			
	Day 3	Finish Reading Chapter 2			
	Day 4	The Big Project			
	Day 5	The Big Project			
Week 4	Day 1	Complete Chapter 2 Vocabulary Terms and Study Questions			

Date	Day	Assignment	Due Date	√	Grade
Week 4	Day 2	Complete Chapter 2 Supply and Demand Exercises			
	Day 3	Complete Chapter 2 Life Integration and Spiritual Application			
	Day 4	The Big Project			
	Day 5	The Big Project			
Week 5	Day 1	Begin Reading Chapter 3			
	Day 2	Continue Reading Chapter 3			
	Day 3	Finish Reading Chapter 3			
	Day 4	The Big Project			
	Day 5	The Big Project			
Week 6	Day 1	Complete Chapter 3 Vocabulary Terms and Study Questions			
	Day 2	Begin Chapter 3 Life-Integration and Spiritual Application			
	Day 3	Finish Chapter 3 Life-Integration and Spiritual Application			
	Day 4	The Big Project			
	Day 5	The Big Project			
Week 7	Day 1	Begin Reading Chapter 4			
	Day 2	Continue Reading Chapter 4			
	Day 3	Finish Reading Chapter 4			
	Day 4	The Big Project			
	Day 5	The Big Project			
Week 8	Day 1	Complete Chapter 4 Vocabulary Terms and Study Questions			
	Day 2	Begin Chapter 4 Life-Integration and Spiritual Application			

Date	Day	Assignment	Due Date	√	Grade
Week 8	Day 3	Finish Chapter 4 Life-Integration and Spiritual Application			
	Day 4	The Big Project			
	Day 5	The Big Project			
Week 9	Day 1	Begin Reading Chapter 5			
	Day 2	Continue Reading Chapter 5			
	Day 3	Finish Reading Chapter 5			
	Day 4	The Big Project			
	Day 5	The Big Project			
First Semester-Second Quarter					
Week 1	Day 1	Complete Chapter 5 Vocabulary Terms			
	Day 2	Begin Chapter 5 Study Questions			
	Day 3	Complete Chapter 5 Study Questions			
	Day 4	The Big Project			
	Day 5	The Big Project			
Week 2	Day 1	Begin Chapter 5 Life Integration and Spiritual Application			
	Day 2	Continue Chapter 5 Life Integration and Spiritual Application			
	Day 3	Finish Chapter 5 Life Integration and Spiritual Application			
	Day 4	The Big Project			
	Day 5	The Big Project			
Week 3	Day 1	Begin Reading Chapter 6			
	Day 2	Continue Reading Chapter 6			

Date	Day	Assignment	Due Date	√	Grade
Week 3	Day 3	Finish Reading Chapter 6			
	Day 4	The Big Project			
	Day 5	The Big Project			
Week 4	Day 1	Complete Chapter 6 Vocabulary Terms			
	Day 2	Begin Chapter 6 Study Questions			
	Day 3	Complete Chapter 6 Study Questions			
	Day 4	The Big Project			
	Day 5	The Big Project			
Week 5	Day 1	Begin Chapter 6 Life Integration and Spiritual Application			
	Day 2	Continue Chapter 6 Life Integration and Spiritual Application			
	Day 3	Finish Chapter 6 Life Integration and Spiritual Application			
	Day 4	The Big Project			
	Day 5	The Big Project			
Week 6	Day 1	Begin Reading Chapter 7			
	Day 2	Continue Reading Chapter 7			
	Day 3	Finish Reading Chapter 7			
	Day 4	The Big Project			
	Day 5	The Big Project			

Date	Day	Assignment	Due Date	√	Grade
Week 7	Day 1	Complete Chapter 7 Vocabulary Terms			
	Day 2	Begin Chapter 7 Study Questions			
	Day 3	Complete Chapter 7 Study Questions			
Week 7	Day 4	The Big Project			
	Day 5	The Big Project			
Week 8	Day 1	Begin Chapter 7 Life Integration and Spiritual Application			
	Day 2	Continue Chapter 7 Life Integration and Spiritual Application			
	Day 3	Finish Chapter 7 Life Integration and Spiritual Application			
	Day 4	The Big Project			
	Day 5	The Big Project			
Week 9	Day 1	Begin Reading Chapter 8			
	Day 2	Continue Reading Chapter 8			
	Day 3	Finish Reading Chapter 8			
	Day 4	The Big Project			
	Day 5	The Big Project			
Mid-Term Grade					

SECOND SEMESTER SUGGESTED DAILY SCHEDULE

Date	Day	Assignment	Due Date	√	Grade
Second Semester–Third Quarter					
Week 1	Day 1	Complete Chapter 8 Vocabulary Terms			
	Day 2	Begin Chapter 8 Study Questions			
	Day 3	Complete Chapter 8 Study Questions			
	Day 4	The Big Project			
	Day 5	The Big Project			
Week 2	Day 1	Begin Chapter 8 Life Integration and Spiritual Application			
	Day 2	Continue Chapter 8 Life Integration and Spiritual Application			
	Day 3	Finish Chapter 8 Life Integration and Spiritual Application			
	Day 4	The Big Project			
	Day 5	The Big Project			
Week 3	Day 1	Begin Reading Chapter 9			
	Day 2	Continue Reading Chapter 9			
	Day 3	Finish Reading Chapter 9			
	Day 4	The Big Project			
	Day 5	The Big Project			
Week 4	Day 1	Complete Chapter 9 Vocabulary Terms			
	Day 2	Begin Chapter 9 Study Questions			
	Day 3	Complete Chapter 9 Study Questions			
	Day 4	The Big Project			

Date	Day	Assignment	Due Date	√	Grade
	Day 5	The Big Project			
Week 5	Day 1	Begin Chapter 9 Life Integration and Spiritual Application			
	Day 2	Continue Chapter 9 Life Integration and Spiritual Application			
	Day 3	Finish Chapter 9 Life Integration and Spiritual Application			
	Day 4	The Big Project			
	Day 5	The Big Project			
Week 6	Day 1	Begin Reading Chapter 10			
	Day 2	Continue Reading Chapter 10			
	Day 3	Finish Reading Chapter 10			
	Day 4	The Big Project			
	Day 5	The Big Project			
Week 7	Day 1	Complete Chapter 10 Vocabulary Terms			
	Day 2	Begin Chapter 10 Study Questions			
	Day 3	Complete Chapter 10 Study Questions			
	Day 4	The Big Project			
	Day 5	The Big Project			
Week 8	Day 1	Begin Chapter 10 Life Integration and Spiritual Application			
	Day 2	Continue Chapter 10 Life Integration and Spiritual Application			
	Day 3	Finish Chapter 10 Life Integration and Spiritual Application			

Date	Day	Assignment	Due Date	√	Grade
Week 8	Day 4	The Big Project			
	Day 5	The Big Project			
Week 9	Day 1	Begin Reading Chapter 11			
	Day 2	Continue Reading Chapter 11			
	Day 3	Finish Reading Chapter 11			
	Day 4	The Big Project			
	Day 5	The Big Project			
Second Semester-Fourth Quarter					
Week 1	Day 1	Begin Chapter 11 Study Questions			
	Day 2	Continue Chapter 11 Study Questions			
	Day 3	Complete Chapter 11 Study Questions			
	Day 4	The Big Project			
	Day 5	The Big Project			
Week 2	Day 1	Begin Chapter 11 Life Integration and Spiritual Application			
	Day 2	Continue Chapter 11 Life Integration and Spiritual Application			
	Day 3	Finish Chapter 11 Life Integration and Spiritual Application			
	Day 4	The Big Project			
	Day 5	The Big Project			
Week 3	Day 1	Begin Reading Chapter 12			
	Day 2	Continue Reading Chapter 12			
	Day 3	Finish Reading Chapter 12			
	Day 4	The Big Project			

Date	Day	Assignment	Due Date	√	Grade
	Day 5	The Big Project			
Week 4	Day 1	Complete Chapter 12 Vocabulary Terms			
	Day 2	Begin Chapter 12 Study Questions			
	Day 3	Complete Chapter 12 Study Questions			
	Day 4	The Big Project			
	Day 5	The Big Project			
Week 5	Day 1	Begin Chapter 12 Life Integration and Spiritual Application			
	Day 2	Continue Chapter 12 Life Integration and Spiritual Application			
	Day 3	Finish Chapter 12 Life Integration and Spiritual Application			
	Day 4	The Big Project			
	Day 5	The Big Project			
Week 6	Day 1	Begin Reading Chapter 13			
	Day 2	Continue Reading Chapter 13			
	Day 3	Finish Reading Chapter 13			
	Day 4	The Big Project			
	Day 5	The Big Project			
Week 7	Day 1	Complete Chapter 13 Vocabulary Terms			
	Day 2	Begin Chapter 13 Study Questions			
	Day 3	Complete Chapter 13 Study Questions			
	Day 4	The Big Project			
	Day 5	The Big Project			

Date	Day	Assignment	Due Date	√	Grade
Week 8	Day 1	Begin Chapter 13 Life Integration and Spiritual Application			
	Day 2	Finish Chapter 13 Life Integration and Spiritual Application			
	Day 3	Study for Final Exam			
	Day 4	The Big Project			
	Day 5	The Big Project			
Week 9	Day 1	Study for Final Exam			
	Day 2	Study for Final Exam			
	Day 3	Complete Final Exam			
	Day 4	The Big Project			
	Day 5	The Big Project			
Final Grade					

1

HUMAN MOTIVATION—WHAT MAKES THE WORLD RUN?

VOCABULARY AND TERMS

The following words or terms appear in the reading. Look up the definitions for each word in the glossary or in a dictionary. Match the word with the correct definition provided below.

_______ 1. Motivation	a. the quantity of a commodity or service wanted at a specified price and time
_______ 2. Repercussions	b. the monetary gain you get from investing capital in a business or effort of some kind
_______ 3. Despair	c. an effect or result, often indirect or remote, that comes from some event or action
_______ 4. Demand	d. a need or desire that encourages a person to act
_______ 5. Profit	e. the worth of something
_______ 6. Value	f. to lose all hope or confidence
_______ 7. Economics	g. money or assets used to start a business on investing in business

________ 8. Prime Mover	h. God, who is the ultimate Cause for all that happens
________ 9. Vanity	i. emptiness or worthlessness
________ 10. Investing	j. to manage somebody else's property
________ 11. Capital	k. the study of how wealth or value is produced, consumed, and transferred
________ 12. Steward	l. Putting your money into something while expecting a profit from it
________ 13. Competition	m. rivalry between people or companies trying to buy or sell more of the same productw

STUDY QUESTIONS

1. How much of the Bible is taken up with the subject of Economics?

____

____

____

2. How is the word "Oikos-despoteo" translated in 1 Timothy 5:14?

____

____

3. How does the world view money or mammon?

4. How will we ever recover from bad economic policies that are destroying our national economies?

5. What is the primary cause behind all of the activity going on in the world? What makes everything function in the world? What part of Romans 11:36 speaks to this?

6. Where does our physical energy come from?

7. What motivates the average man of the world to get out of bed in the morning?

8. What happens to men of the world who lose motivation to make money and build their kingdoms?

9. What do typical people in the world hope for?

10. What is the Christian's highest goal or purpose in life?

____

____

____

11. What is the strongest driving force in the world?

____

____

____

12. Jesus said, "You cannot serve God and ________________________."

13. What is our identity in relation to Jesus Christ (as Christians)? In your own words, explain how your identity is tied into your motivation for getting out of bed and getting things done.

____

____

____

14. How do we look at our paychecks or money rewards received (as Christians)?

____

____

15. What are the three steps to supplying a demand?

LIFE INTEGRATION AND SPIRITUAL APPLICATION

1. If you are a young man, what does 1 Timothy 5:8 mean for your life?

If you are a young woman, what does 1 Timothy 5:14 and Titus 2:5 mean for your life?

2. What is expected of a son or daughter for six days per week in Exodus 20:9-11? What is expected of a son or daughter on one day per week?

3. Read Ecclesiastes 2:9-11.

What was Solomon's conclusion concerning all of the pleasure, all of his wealth, and all of his accomplishments in life (according to verse 11)?

4. Read Ecclesiastes 2:21-23.

How much reward does a man get for his work? What about the man who is a workaholic? How does Solomon describe this man's fulfillment?

5. Read Ecclesiastes 5:10-17.

What is the end effect on the person who loves silver (money)?

What does the rich man lose, according to verse 12?

What can you take with you when you die (of everything you have purchased or earned) according to verse 15?

6. What is the whole conclusion to the matter, as recorded in Ecclesiastes 12:13?

7. Study the Parable of the Wise Steward in Luke 16:1-13 once more.

Why was the rich landowner happy with the steward?

Whose money and resources are we stewarding as Christians?

What does God want you to do with the resources He has given you? How would you apply the steward's example to your life?

8. Read the following taken from 1 Timothy 6:9-10. "But those who desire to be rich fall into temptation and a snare, and into many foolish and harmful lusts which drown men in destruction and perdition. For the love of money is a root of all kinds of evil, for which some have strayed from the faith in their greediness, and pierced themselves through with many sorrows."

What are the two human tendencies that are so dangerous as described here?

9. What are the two resources that God has given you?

Where are you investing your time? Over the next week, take an inventory of your time usage. How do you spend your 110 waking hours each week? Fill in the following table.

HOW DO YOU SPEND YOUR 110 WAKING HOURS?

	Ideal	Actual
1. Personal Bible Reading and Prayer		
2. Family Worship		
3. Church Meetings/Bible Studies		
4. Study/School		
5. Work /Making Money		
6. Preparing Food		
7. Shopping		
8. Eating		
9. Personal Hygiene		
10. Travel		
11. Listening to the Word - Good Spiritual Music while Traveling		
12. Cleaning House/Chores		
13. Serving Widows/ Brothers and Sisters in Church		
14. Extra Reading		
15. Entertainment /Recreation		

10. Which of the following motivations are stronger with you?

a. The motivation to compete with somebody else for money or rewards

b. The motivation to serve somebody, to bless somebody, to relieve suffering

____

____

c. The motivation to serve the Lord Jesus Christ

____

2 THE LAWS OF SUPPLY AND DEMAND

VOCABULARY AND TERMS

The following words or terms appear in the reading. Look up the definitions for each word in the glossary or in a dictionary. Match the word with the correct definition provided below.

________ 1. Supply	a. the customers' evaluation of the merits of a product or service
________ 2. Investment	b. the management of revenues; the conduct or transaction of money matters generally, especially those affecting the public, as in the fields of banking and investment
________ 3. Perdition	c. Some things which are needful for life and have practical benefit to human life
________ 4. Real Useful Value	d. the state or quality of being useful; usefulness
________ 5. Perceived Useful Value	e. utter destruction or ruin
________ 6. Exchange Value	f. preoccupation with or emphasis on material objects, comforts, and considerations, with a disinterest in or rejection of spiritual values
________ 7. Market	g. organizing and managing any enterprise, especially a business, usually with considerable initiative and risk

________ 8. Materialism	h. insufficiency or shortness of supply; dearth
________ 9. Mammon	i. the course of commercial activity by which the exchange of commodities is affected: extent of demand
________ 10. Utility	j. a quantity of something on hand or available, as for use; a stock or store
________ 11. Scarcity	k. all the features and characteristics of a product or service that bear on its ability to satisfy customers' needs or expectations; the degree of excellence in the product or service
________ 12. Trade	l. to offer goods or services at an unreasonably lower price or rate than a competing price or rate
________ 13. Finance	m. the chance that an investment will lose value
________ 14. Undercutting Market	n. the services performed by workers for wages
________ 15. Quality	o. a source of supply or support: a natural source of wealth or revenue
________ 16. Resources	p. the act or process of buying, selling, or exchanging commodities, at either wholesale or retail, within a country or between countries
________ 17. Labor	q. value set on a product by the market
________ 18. Risk	r. the outlay of money usually for income or profit
________ 19. Entrepreneurship	s. material wealth or possessions especially as having a debasing influence

STUDY QUESTIONS

1. What are some examples of things that are needful in life?

2. What would you consider to be luxuries? What would people living in 1910 consider to be luxuries?

3. What sorts of things have a perceived useful value, but lack the value once the thing is purchased?

4. What is the exchange value for a 2015 Toyota Camry SE for sale in your city? What is the market price right now for the car, as advertised in a newspaper, magazine, or online? Find three examples and take the average price. (The student should access these resources with oversight from a parent/teacher.)

5. From the list given in the text on pages 17–19, what are the influences that increase demand in the following examples? (More than one may apply.)

a. Demand for Vitamin C in the winter time
b. Demand for T-shirts with the Superbowl or World Cup team winner emblazoned on it
c. Demand for automatic garage openers
d. Demand for playing the lottery when signs indicate the winnings are $10 billion

6. What is covetousness?

7. What are the unhealthy elements driving market demands?

8. What is a good indication that a spoiled kid has been getting too many treats or luxuries?

9. Why is an auction a good place to determine the value of something?

10. What is a "free market trade?"

11. When people are bargaining in the open market, what does the seller want? What does the buyer want?

12. What are the factors that tie into the pricing of a used car?

13. Why does supply rise when the price of a product goes up in a given market?

14. Why does demand go down, when the price of a product goes up in a given market?

15. What is market equilibrium?

16. What is elasticity? Give an example of a product with high elasticity as well as a product with low elasticity.

17. What did Malthus forget about when he got people worried about the world running out of food?

18. What are the four things you need in order to supply the world with a product they can purchase and use?

19. How much labor cost does it take to build a house, a car, or a table, or a deck? Do the math on the following table, given the average hours and hourly wage costs provided. You might use a different hourly wage if you live in a different country.

Product	Hours to Make It	Hourly Wage	Labor Costs
House (2000 sq. ft., 186 sq. m.)	2,400 hours	$16.36	
Automobile, assembly	30 hours	$16.36	
Kitchen Table	8 hours	$16.36	
Deck (300 sq ft. 28 sq. m.)	120 hours	$16.36	

20. What ultimately governs the success of our work? Who brings forth the increase?

SUPPLY AND DEMAND EXERCISES

1. Produce a Supply-Demand Chart for Lemonade in Your City

Prices will range from $1.00 to $6.00 for 16 ounces of Lemonade.
Quantities will range from 0 - 500

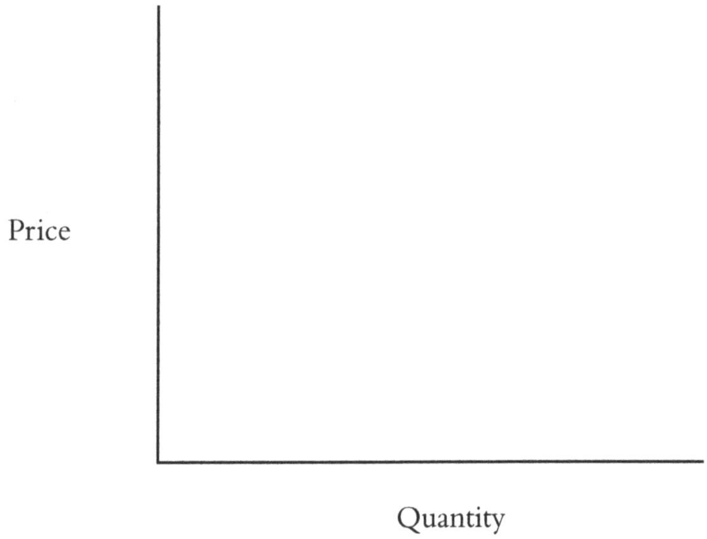

The Lemonade Stand Inc. says that they are willing to produce the following quantities of lemonade at the associated prices. Draw the Supply Line on the Graph above.

Price/Unit	Cups of Lemonade
$1.00	175
$2.00	225
$3.00	300
$4.00	350
$5.00	425

After testing out the market, the Lemonade businesses have learned that people are willing to buy lemonade at the following prices.

Price/Unit	Cups of Lemonade
$1.00	500
$2.00	425
$3.00	350
$4.00	225
$5.00	175

Shade in the area of Shortage

Shade in the area for Surplus

a. At a price of $1.00 would there be a surplus or a shortage? ______________

b. How many units under or over? ______________

c. At a price of $4.00 would there be a surplus or shortage? ______________

d. How many units under or over? ______________

e. Where is the equilibrium? ______________

2. Fill in the following chart for elasticity of price. Remember elasticity is the measurement of change in demand divided by the measurement of change in price. Anything under 1.0 is inelastic. Anything over 1.0 is elastic. State whether the product is elastic or inelastic.

Product	Demand Change	Price Change	Elasticity	Elastic or Inelastic?
Luxury Diamonds	-5%	30%		
Gas	10%	-30%		
Salt	-10%	20%		
Instant Coffee	50%	30%		
Baked Beans	100%	-25%		
Financial Magazine	-30%	10%		

LIFE INTEGRATION AND SPIRITUAL APPLICATION

1. Read Matthew 7:12 again (the Golden Rule). What is at least one way this might apply to how you treat competitors or how to treat customers in business?

____

____

____

2. Consider Proverbs 23:19–21 and 1 Timothy 6:6–8. What are the indications that you have given way to sin with materials, luxuries, and pleasures of this world?

____

____

____

3. Consider the warning in 1 Timothy 6:9-10. What is your view of money? Are you drawn to getting rich? Is your foot anywhere near this trap - the trap of the love of money?

____

____

____

4. Consider 1 Thessalonians 5:18: "In everything give thanks; for this is the will of God in Christ Jesus for you."

Do you thank God for your meals? ____________________

Do you thank God for your snacks? ____________________

Do you thank God for your hard trials? ____________________

Do you thank God for your school subjects that are really hard? ____________________

Do you thank God for your parents? ____________________

Do you thank God for your siblings (if you have brothers or sisters)? ____________________

Do you thank God for your church? ____________________

What are the things you do not thank God for?

____

____

____

____

5. Are there any material things you want to buy? Why do you want to buy these things? Do you think that these are good reasons or bad reasons?

6. Is there an idol in your life? Is there something you love more than God? What would that be?

3 WEALTH INEQUALITY - WHY SOME NATIONS ARE RICH AND OTHERS ARE POOR

VOCABULARY AND TERMS

The following words or terms appear in the reading. Look up the definitions for each word in the glossary or in a dictionary. Match the word with the correct definition provided below.

_______ 1. Macroeconomy	a. Intending to do what is right, especially to do one's work or duty with a high sense of quality, carefully and thoroughly
_______ 2. Microeconomy	b. characterized by lack of seriousness or sense
_______ 3. Efficiency	c. government system(s) characterized by specialization of functions, adherence to fixed rules, and a hierarchy of authority
_______ 4. Civil government	d. one individual's or one household's participation in the economy
_______ 5. Bureaucracy	e. the outlay of money usually with the intention of producing income or profit
_______ 6. Economy	f. the practical implementation of a state on behalf of its citizens
_______ 7. Investment	g. being without a usual, typical, or expected attribute or accompaniment

________ 8. Conscientiousness	h. the ability to do something or produce something without wasting materials, time, or energy
________ 9. Devoid	i. all the activity of a household, a community, or a country, etc., usually referring to the financial business of producing, buying, and selling; the management of this human activity
________ 10. Frivolous	j. a state of being under obligation to pay or repay someone or something in return for something received: a state of servant-hood or slavery
________ 11. Debt	k. all the work, all the buying and selling, and all the useful things made by a whole nation of people working together
________ 12. Supercilious	l. the practical implementation of a state on behalf of its citizens

STUDY QUESTIONS

1. What is the ultimate reason why some nations are richer (and more productive) than others?

2. What happens to nations that turn towards immorality in a big way, according to Deuteronomy 28:15-19?

3. What is the work to rest ratio that God has commanded for us?

4. What is the second most important contributor to a productive economy?

5. Suppose you pay a carpenter $20 per hour to build your house. If it takes him 200 hours to secure every nail in an averaged sized house using a hammer, and only two hours, using a nail gun, how much money do you save if the carpenter uses a nail gun?

How much money is saved on the 500,000 new homes built each year in the US?

If the average nail gun costs $250, how much money do you save if you buy a nail gun to build one home?

6. What does it mean to work “smart?”

7. How do corrupt governments slow down the economy?

8. Why did people have a hard time inventing and building automobiles in 1700?

9. What are some of the most important inventions that made farming and carpentry more efficient?

____

____

____

10. How much did the mass production of nails cut the price of nails? When did the first mass production of nails begin?

____

____

____

11. Who owns the world and everything in it? Do unbelievers agree with this? Who owns the world and everything in it, according to them (do you think)?

____

____

____

12. What is our relationship with or responsibility in relation to the land, the animals, the trees, and the crops?

13. Which of the ten commandments establishes a person's right to own something, such that others should not take it from him?

14. What happens to investments when the owner doesn't take good care of them? What happens when you don't maintain your car? What happens when you don't maintain your house?

15. What are higher blessings or better blessings than wealth?

16. Where do the whiniest people in the world live?

17. As described in the example provided under Principle #6, how does the apple merchant cheat? How does the buyer cheat?

18. What is the root of all kinds of evil?

19. How does God look at get-rich-quick schemes? Give several examples of these schemes.

20. What happens when we fail to keep the Sabbath and go without a day of rest in the week?

21. What can we say about nations like the United States and Japan that are deep in debt?

____

____

____

____

22. The following table looks at the 11 worst and 11 best countries for debt (out of 185 countries in the world). Take a look at the table below and answer the following questions:

a. Which country is doing the worst in the world as measured by debt?

b. Which is the 11th worst country in the world as measured by debt?

c. What is the best country in the world as measured by debt?

d. Of the highest population countries (over 100 million people), which country is doing the best?

Which country is doing the worst?

Name	National Debt to GDP Ratio	Population
Japan	237.54%	125,584,838
Venezuela	214.45%	29,266,991
Sudan	177.87%	43,000,000
Greece	174.15%	10,316,637
Lebanon	157.81%	6,684,849
Italy	133.43%	60,262,770
Eritrea	127.34%	3,662,244
Mozambique	124.46%	33,089,461
Portugal	119.46%	10,140,570
Singapore	109.37%	5,943,546
United States	106.70%	334,805,269
Paraguay	22.37%	7,305,843
Luxembourg	21.61%	642,371
Zimbabwe	20.99%	15,331,428
Kazakhstan	20.90%	19,205,043
Bulgaria	19.33%	6,844,597
United Arab Emirates	19.20%	10,081,785
DR Congo	14.01%	95,240,792
Russia	13.79%	145,805,947
Botswana	12.78%	2,441,162
Estonia	7.61%	1,321,910
Afghanistan	6.88%	40,754,388

LIFE INTEGRATION AND SPIRITUAL APPLICATION

1. What are some of the ways that you waste time when you are supposed to be working?

2. Consider the reasons why poor countries remain poor on pages 39 and 40. Which of these problems afflict your country, do you think?

3. What has God made you responsible over in your life?

   How much money do you have?

   Do you have a bed, a closet, and a dresser?

What are your responsibilities in the home?

What are your talents?

4. Review Colossians 3:22-24. Who does every single Christian work for? What is our attitude while we work (according to this passage)?

5. Consider Proverbs 13:11. What happens to those who gain wealth by dishonesty?

6. What should you consider first before you try to get more money, more business, and more stuff?

7. What are the two kinds of slothfulness described in Proverbs 22:13 and Proverbs 12:27? Which of these forms do you give in to? In what situations might you give way to this slothfulness?

8. What percentage of a person's income was required for the tithe to the temple in the Old Testament? What does God say of people who give less than that amount (in Malachi 3:8)? How much should you tithe of the money you earn?

THORNS AND THISTLES - THE REALITY OF SIN, THE EFFECTS OF SIN, AND JUDGMENT

4

VOCABULARY AND TERMS

The following words or terms appear in the reading. Look up the definitions for each word in the glossary or in a dictionary. Match the word with the correct definition provided below.

________ 1. Entropy	a. a rise in prices usually related to an increase in the volume of money in an economy and the loss of value with the currency
________ 2. Subsistence Farming	b. government by the people; a system of governance in which the people vote for their leaders
________ 3. Common Grace	c. lacking the qualities or abilities needed for effective action: inadequate to or unsuitable for a particular purpose
________ 4. Incompetent	d. to release from slavery or servitude
________ 5. Profit	e. farming whose products are intended to provide for the basic needs of the farmer, with little surplus for marketing
________ 6. Jubilee	f. no longer used because something newer exists

________ 7. Manumission	g. government characterized by specialization of functions, adherence to fixed rules, and a hierarchy of authority
________ 8. Inflation	h. a period of economic contraction, sometimes limited in scope or duration
________ 9. Recession	i. the state of being poor
________ 10. Obsolete	j. monetary gain resulting from the employment of capital in any transaction, the difference between the amount spent and the amount earned
________ 11. Democracy	k. a year of emancipation and restoration provided, to be kept every 50 years, by the emancipation of the enslaved, restoration of alienated lands to their former owners, and omission of all cultivation of the land
________ 12. Bureaucracy	l. the degradation or decay of matter and energy in the universe
________ 13. Impoverishment	m. God's indiscriminate kindness and mercy which preserve all men, believers and unbelievers, through the abundant and daily blessings of earthly life

STUDY QUESTIONS

1. What did the fall do for man's work life?

____

____

2. What would happen to a house that wasn't taken care of over a period of twenty years?

3. What has caused most of the recent famines in the last century?

4. What has caused famines in Africa?

5. How much grain does the US consume per year? How much does the nation keep in storage? How long would this last if the nation experienced a really bad drought?

6. What percentage of the world population died of starvation in the 20th century (approximately)?

7. How does God's common grace keep people from starving to death?

8. What are some of the negative consequences of man's fall into sin?

9. What was the maximum length allowed for enslavement of the Israelites in the Old Testament?

10. While Christians were redeeming the slaves, what group of people were getting more involved in the slave trade (in the 8th–11th centuries)? Who did they enslave?

11. Which Roman Catholic Pope revived slavery? Which Roman Catholic kings of England initiated the slave trade to the American colonies?

12. What Christian evangelical worked hard to get rid of slavery in the late 1700s?

____

____

____

13. How do we get rid of slavery?

____

____

____

____

14. Why should a man borrow money according to Deuteronomy 15?

____

____

____

15. Why do rich people want to go into debt?

____

____

16. If a businessman buys a house for $200,000 with a down payment of $20,000, how much does he have to borrow to make the purchase?

If inflation causes the price of the house to go up to $250,000 in 2 years, how much money does he add to his $20,000 down payment? How much money did he make by inflation?

If deflation causes the price of the house to go down to $150,000, and he sells the house at $150,000, how much money did he lose? How much money does he have to pay the bank out of his own pocket?

17. How does Proverbs 28:15 describe a wicked ruler? What does this say of bad government leaders?

18. How many righteous men could have saved Sodom and Gomorrah? How many Christians might save Los Angeles from God's judgment, based on a similar ratio?

19. Which nations are the most honest and the most prosperous nations in the world? What is the faith that has predominated in these countries?

20. How do prosperous nations built up on free enterprise tend to break down?

LIFE INTEGRATION AND SPIRITUAL APPLICATION

1. Consider Genesis 9:25. How can we deduce from this passage that slavery is a curse?

2. What creates big government according to Proverbs 28:2? How can you prevent big government from developing in your nation?

3. Read over Psalm 112 once more. What are the blessings that attend a man who fears the Lord?

What are the characteristics of this man?

Which of these characteristics do you desire to emulate?

4. Read Psalm 72 about the coming of David's Son, the Lord Jesus Christ. What are the blessings He brings to a world of sin and corruption? Do you think that Jesus and His people (Christians) have made the world better over the last 2,000 years?

5. What was the motto coined during the Great Depression? Have you lived by this rule?

____

____

____

ECONOMIC THEORIES - BIBLICAL ECONOMICS AND THE ECONOMIC SYSTEMS OF MEN

5

VOCABULARY AND TERMS

The following words or terms appear in the reading. Look up the definitions for each word in the glossary or in a dictionary. Match the word with the correct definition provided below.

_______ 1. Feudalism	a. a person empowered to decide matters at issue; judge; umpire
_______ 2. Capitalism	b. a part of something; a component
_______ 3. Socialism	c. a social system that existed in Europe during the Middle Ages in which people worked and fought for nobles who gave them protection and the use of land in return
_______ 4. Communism	d. a social theory advocating the liberty rights, or independent action, of the individual: the pursuit of individual rather than common or collective interests
_______ 5. Distributism	e. God's original plan for economic stewardship of His creation, where the family works together in reliance upon the Lord, each other, and other families in their community. They do not rely on governments and corporations
_______ 6. Family Economy	f. an economy in which there are elements of both public and private enterprise

________ 7. Magna Carta	g. the political principle of centralized social and economic control, especially of all means of production
________ 8. Constituent	h. the theory or practice of distributing private property (as land) to the maximum degree among individual owners/families
________ 9. Corporation	i. a pamphlet (1848) by Karl Marx and Friedrich Engels: the first statement of the principles of modern communism
________ 10. Mixed Economies	j. the theory, policy, or practice of lessening or reducing inequalities in income through such measures as progressive income taxation and antipoverty programs
________ 11. Communist Manifesto	k. a legal entity formed by a group of one or more investors
________ 12. Arbiter	l. a system of social organization in which all economic and social activity is controlled by a totalitarian state dominated by a single and self-perpetuating political party
________ 13. Redistribution	m. an economic system in which investment in and ownership of the means of production, distribution, and exchange of wealth is made and maintained chiefly by private individuals or corporations, especially as contrasted to cooperatively or state-owned means of wealth
________ 14. Individualism	n. the "great charter" of English liberties, forced from King John by the English barons and sealed at Runnymede, June 15, 1215
________ 15. Collectivism	o. a theory or system of social organization that advocates the ownership and control of the means of production and distribution, capital, land, etc., by the community as a whole, usually through a centralized government

STUDY QUESTIONS

1. What are the strategies the Persians, Greeks, and Romans used to increase their revenues and become great empires?

2. What were the biblical principles that changed the world economy after Jesus came?

3. What was the system of economy that developed in Europe after the fall of Rome?

4. How did the serfs differ from slaves? Was it better than the old world's economic system of slavery?

5. What was the governmental structure of these kingdoms?

6. What is the motive that creates national wealth, according to Adam Smith? Is this the fundamental motive for Christians in their work and service?

7. Who owns businesses in a capitalist economy?

8. What was the fundamental shift that occurred in the Industrial Revolution?

9. According to the US Census Bureau, there were 128,000,000 households in the US in 2020, and 24,300,000 households in 1920. The number of family farms in the US declined from 6,500,000 (in 1920) to 2,000,000 (in 2020). What was the decline in percentage of American households that worked a family farm between 1920 and 2020?

10. Where does capitalism fall short?

11. Identify the following descriptions with the term that best applies: Capitalism, Communism, or Socialism.

a. Believes that man is innately good.

____

b. Calls for the total abolition of private property.

____

c. The goal of socialism is

____

d. Stands for the right to free trade between free traders.

____

e. Undermined the family economy in the 1700s and early 1800s.

____

f. Deifies man and dethrones God.

____

g. Seeks to equalize wealth in a society by gradual reforms rather than revolution.

____

12. Take a look at the chart comparing the average income for people living in the United States to people living in Cuba, a communist country that claims to be an equal society.

a. How much does the average (median) family in America earn per year (as of the year AD 2000)?

____

b. How much does the average family in Cuba earn per year?

____

c. What is the ratio?

____

13. If distributism does not involve a family farm, what does distributism look like in the modern world?

____

____

____

14. Who owns the factories and farms in a communist economy? Who owns the factories and farms in a capitalist economy? Who owns the factories and farms in a distributist economy?

____

____

____

____

15. What are the two basic parts of the family economy?

16. What are the elements of the family economy (the things that families do)?

17. Which of the three economic systems are most helpful to the family economy? Which is the most hurtful?

18. What did Karl Marx say about the family?

19. What was Karl Marx's objective in life (in his own words)?

20. How does capitalism help or hurt the family?

21. What happens to child care in capitalist societies? What happens to elder care in capitalist societies?

22. Which system emphasizes what? Match the following:

a. Socialism	Efficiency
b. Capitalism	Love and Relationships
c. Biblical Economics	Equality

23. Why do you think liberty is dependent on property ownership, owning your own business, and running family economies?

24. What are the benefits of a family economy?

LIFE INTEGRATION AND SPIRITUAL APPLICATION

1. As you consider the world's values of "equality," "wealth," "efficiency," etc., what are your highest values in life? What are the things that are most important to you in life? What biblical backing do you have for these values?

2. Study Acts 2:44-45. Compare with Acts 5:1-4. What is the difference between socialism and the practice of the early church? In what sorts of situations might we do the same thing the early church did?

3. Suppose you owned large factories with 1,000 employees working for you. Based on 1 Timothy 6:17-19 and similar scriptures, how would you handle your money? How could you encourage more distributism? How could you strengthen the families of those working for you?

6 GETTING YOUR JOB - WORK IN THE ECONOMY

VOCABULARY AND TERMS

The following words or terms appear in the reading. Look up the definitions for each word in the glossary or in a dictionary. Match the word with the correct definition provided below.

_______ 1. Work

_______ 2. Entrepreneurship

_______ 3. Apprenticeship

_______ 4. Contract Labor

_______ 5. Partnership

_______ 6. Corporation

_______ 7. Investment

a. labor coercible by the enforceable provisions of a contract

b. a state of being under obligation to pay or repay someone or something in return for something received: a state of owing

c. a legal entity formed by a group of one or more investors

d. to distribute the administrative powers or functions of (a central authority) over a less concentrated area; localized control

e. the practice of working from home, making use of the internet, email, and the telephone

f. a government enforced monopoly to unify and increase the power and especially the monetary wealth of a nation by a strict governmental regulation of the entire national economy, usually through policies designed to secure an accumulation of bullion

g. organizing and managing any enterprise, especially a business, usually with considerable initiative and risk

_______ 8. Mercantilism	h. a particular market where stocks and bonds are traded; stock exchange
_______ 9. Stock Market	i. a contract by which a person, as an apprentice, is bound to service
_______ 10. Debt	j. any insolvent debtor; a person unable to satisfy any just claims made upon him or her. Utter ruin, failure, depletion, or the like: utter impoverishment
_______ 11. Bankruptcy	k. basic principle for all of learning where an individual applies, puts into practice, and has a hands-on experience of the important principles he or she learned
_______ 12. Indenture	l. a method of distributing products or services in which a party pays a fee and/or royalties to use the brand's trademark, trade name, and business approach
_______ 13. Franchise	m. the outlay of money, usually for income or profit
_______ 14. Decentralize	n. a legal relation existing between two or more persons who are contractually associated as joint principals in a business
_______ 15. Life Integration	o. to perform or carry through a task requiring sustained effort or continuous, repeated operations; a matter of taking dominion of God's world and providing for human needs
_______ 16. Telecommuting	p. the state in which a person is committed to working for somebody else without regular pay
_______ 17. Bond Slavery	q. a program or position in which someone learns a trade by working under a certified expert

STUDY QUESTIONS

1. What percentage of the world is self-employed? What percent of Americans are self employed?

2. What is God's expectation in terms of how we spend our time during the week?

3. How do economists define work? How is work defined in a biblical context? What is the difference?

4. What is good or effective work?

5. What is the difference between ministry work and business work?

6. What were the effects of the depreciation of motherhood?

7. List 5-6 different kinds of business work.

8. What kind of business ownership might the following make-believe or real companies represent (of the 4 listed in the text)?
   a. Joe's Plumbing

   ____

   b. Waldron Family's Walmart

   ____

   c. Chick-fil-A in your town

   ____

   d. IBM stock

   ____

   e. Jimmy's Lemonade Stand

   ____

   f. Dr. Krak's Chiropractic Office

   ____

9. What is the difference between common stock and preferred stock?

____

____

____

10. How does God's law advocate free trade and a fair playing field?

11. How could debt and incorporation (and selling stock) help you to get rich quick?

12. In what way(s) was Rockefeller's road to success legitimate?

13. If the wicked borrows and doesn't repay, what is the most honest form of bankruptcy?

14. Critical Thinking Question: What is the difference between entrepreneurship and self-employment?

15. What are the four benefits of self-employment?

16. What are the four drawbacks of self-employment?

17. What is your most important goal when you are working at a job?

LIFE INTEGRATION AND SCRIPTURAL APPLICATION

1. What are the four big time-wasters in the workplace?

Which of these traps are you more likely to fall into?

What is a good remedy to keep you from falling into this trap?

2. Consider Exodus 22:6. According to God's law, who is responsible for making restitution for the damage done by the fire? By this standard, who should be held responsible when a company's negligence results in death (as in the case of the Bhopal India disaster)?

3. Read Psalm 37:21. How does the wicked borrow without the intention of paying off the loans in our present day?

4. Are you an entrepreneur? How would you answer these questions?

Yes or No

______ Are you a self-starter?

______ Do you like to do things your own way?

______ Are you self-motivated enough that you don't need anybody to tell you what to do each day?

______ Are you able to motivate others to follow you? Do people like to follow your ideas?

______ Are you the kind of person who likes to take charge?

______ Do you want to make sure that the project gets completed or do you get discouraged and just walk away?

______ Can you keep going when the going gets tough?

______ Are you a super-hard worker even when work is difficult? Will you make sure the job gets done no matter how hard it might be?

______ Can you make quick decisions with wise input from others?

______ Are you able to take risks and make mistakes without worrying too much about failure?

If you answered yes to 8 out of 10 of these questions, you are probably an entrepreneur.

5. Read Romans 12:3. Take a moment and think "soberly" about your own strengths and weaknesses. Suppose you were applying for a lawn maintenance job. How would you rate yourself on the following items? If you are very weak in this area, put a 1 in the blank space. If you are very strong in this area, put a 10 in the blank space. (Again, you should be humble and honest—thinking soberly about yourself.)

____ I am knowledgeable about lawn maintenance.

____ I am polite and respectful to customers and to managers on the job.

____ I am honest. I tell the truth even when it is difficult.

____ I am creative. I come up with good solutions to do a better job.

_____ I am conscientious and always try to do quality work.

_____ I work fast. I am not lazy.

_____ I don't give up. I work on problems until I get it figured out.

_____ I am ambitious. I want to excel in what I do, and then take on more responsibility.

_____ I am dependable, reliable, and responsible. My parents or my supervisors don't have to tell me what to do. I just get the job done.

_____ I get along well with people. In fact, I try to resolve conflicts that other people have with each other.

_____ I don't complain. I maintain a positive attitude most of the time.

_____ I am skilled at lawn maintenance.

6. Find a Bible verse that speaks to these characteristics of a good employee.

a. Work hard and put your heart into the work.

____

b. Honor your manager.

____

c. Don't speak negatively of your fellow employees.

____

d. Be honest. Don't hide problems that develop in the job.

e. Don't be a people pleaser in the work place.

f. Be humble. Be a good listener.

7. As you seek God's calling on your life, have you been faithful to the following?

a. Have you sought to know God more in your present situation. Are you in His will right now?

b. Have you prayed for wisdom?

c. Have you prepared for the general things God requires of a man or a woman?

d. Have you sought counsel?

e. Have you gained some experience by working different jobs?

8. Have you overcome laziness or lack of direction in your life? How might you change your habits in the following areas? Choose at least one of these actions and follow through with it.

a. Ask the Holy Spirit for the gift of self-control.

b. Develop a long-term vision for your life. What are some goals you would like to accomplish, considering your talents and abilities?

____

____

____

c. Schedule each week ahead of time, laying out specific priorities and goals you would like to get done.

d. Take fifteen minutes each morning to lay out the priorities and goals you would like to get done for that day. Keep your list in front of you throughout the day.

e. Put your electronic devices and distractions away for long periods of time. Throw away your smartphone if it is hindering you from completing your work.

f. Eat healthily. Get sufficient sleep.

g. Obey the fourth commandment and establish a regular habit of resting one day in seven.

7 BANKING AND YOUR MONEY-HOW THE WORLD ROBS, CHEATS, AND STEALS

VOCABULARY AND TERMS

The following words or terms appear in the reading. Look up the definitions for each word in the glossary or in a dictionary. Match the word with the correct definition provided below.

________ 1. Trade	a. a particular market where stocks and bonds are traded
________ 2. Barter Economy	b. the total amount of money contained in US checking accounts, coins, and currencies
________ 3. Miserliness	c. a type of cryptocurrency popular in the 2020s
________ 4. Counterfeit	d. of, like, or befitting a person who lives in wretched circumstances in order to save and hoard money
________ 5. Cryptocurrencies	e. the act or process of buying, selling, or exchanging commodities, at either wholesale or retail, within a country or between countries
________ 6. Bitcoin	f. a sum paid or charged for the use of money or for borrowing money
________ 7. Deposit	g. the value of all the goods and services produced within a country (usually over a period of a year)

________ 8. Interest	h. an insurance intended to protect a client's property in case it is damaged during maintenance or servicing
________ 9.Judicious	i. to place for safekeeping or in trust, especially in a bank account; to give as security or in part payment
________ 10. Bonding	j. made as an imitation so as to be passed off fraudulently or deceptively as genuine; forged
________ 11. Stock Market	k. an economy where exchange of commodities is solely based upon trades, rather than by the use of money
________ 12. Inflation	l. any form of currency that only exists digitally, which usually has no central issuing or regulating authority, but instead uses a decentralized system to record transactions and manage the issuance of new units, and then relies on cryptography to prevent counterfeiting and fraudulent transactions
________ 13. M1 Money Supply	m. having, exercising, or characterized by sound judgment
________ 14. Gross Domestic Product (GDP)	n. all things that have a monetary or exchange value, or anything that has utility and is capable of being appropriated or exchanged
________ 15. Wealth	o. a persistent, substantial rise in the general level of prices related to an increase in the volume of money, resulting in the loss of currency value
________ 16. Fractional Reserve Banking	p. a practice in which banks will lend out more money than that which they hold in reserve

STUDY QUESTIONS

1. What is money?

____

____

____

2. Fill in each blank in the following table for each type of money considered with a Yes or No. If the type of money considered is scarce, then write "Yes" under "Scarcity." If the type of money considered is not scarce, then write "No" under "Scarcity."

Type of Money	Price Stability	Scarcity	Universal Desirability	Divisibility	Portability	Durability
Paper						
Fish						
Gold						
Silver						
Pianos						
Salt						
Crypto-currency						

3. What are the uses of money? List at least two.

____

____

4. Why is it a bad idea to bury tools in the ground? What does this have to do with money?

5. How much gold would it take to rent a 4-room flat in Wichita Kansas in 2020?

How much gold would it take to rent a 4-room flat in America in 1880?

How much gold would it take to rent a 4-room flat in London in 1768?

6. If a shekel is 1/4 ounce of silver, and silver is valued at $25.00 an ounce (in 2022), how much silver and how much in dollars did Abraham pay for the Cave of Machpelah?

7. Between the years 1837 and 1866, how many different kinds of currency or coin were issued by different people in America?

8. What are the three ways to cheat in a trade?

9. How did deceitful people reduce the value of silver and gold coins in past history?

10. Who are the people who are advantaged by this deceitful debasement of money? Who are the people who are most hurt by it?

11. What is the crime known as "bouncing a check"?

12. What was the purpose of paper money when it first came into use?

13. When did the French government get into the counterfeiting business (with the assistance of a murderer by the name of John Law)? Who was the King that gave approval for this?

14. When did the US finally give up on the gold standard?

15. How do banks make their money?

16. If you borrow $150,000 from a bank at 10% interest rate, how much money would you pay in interest for the first year? How much would you pay per month (for the interest)?

17. If the saver puts $150,000 into the bank at 2% interest, how much money does he get from the bank in a year? If the bank is lending the money at 10% and the bank is giving the saver $2%, how much profit does the bank make from your money in a year?

18. What were the special advantages given to the first US national bank?

19. Why did the "Run on the Bank" happen in 1819?

20. What was the year that the Federal Reserve Notes were no longer redeemable by gold "on demand"?

21. What was the year that the US Treasury stopped issuing silver certificates that were redeemable in silver? Why was this deceitful?

____

____

____

22. What are three tools the Federal Reserve uses to manipulate the value of money in circulation?

____

____

____

23. How much did the US household debt increase (as a percentage of the GDP) from 1980 to 2020?

____

____

____

____

How much did the US business debt increase (as a percentage of the GDP) from 1980 to 2020?

____

____

____

How much did the US federal government debt increase (as a percentage of the GDP) from 1980 to 2020?

____

____

____

24. How much did the wealthiest 0.01% of Americans benefit by this debt and an inflationary economy between 1980 and 2020? Fill in the percentage of wealth owned by the wealthiest Americans by year (below).

1980 __________

2008 __________

2021__________

25. How did companies artificially inflate the value of their own stock in the 2000s?

____

____

26. How much did Apple Computer invest in their own stock in 2021? How much did Apple's stock value increase between 2019 and 2021?

27. Fill in the following chart and compare the average income and prices in the American economy between 1930 and 2020. Calculate each ratio.

	1930	2020	Ratio
Gallon of Milk			
Gallon of Gas			
Average Income			

28. What explains the rise in income as well as the rise in prices for Milk and Gas (between 1930 and 2020)?

29. Referring to the inflation allegory, answer the following questions:

a. How much money was in the little community at the beginning?

---

b. How much money did the king print?

---

c. How much money did he keep for himself?

---

d. How much money did the king hand out to the community?

---

e. Why were the people so happy to receive the money from the king?

---

f. How much money (in original value) was stolen from each person after the king printed the money and provided the hand outs to the community?

---

30. How much quantitative easing (money printing) occurred between 2008 and 2021?

---

31. Consider the second allegory concerning the king who took advantage of money printing and answer these questions.

a. How much money was in the community before the king (and his thugs) started printing money?

---

b. How much money did the thugs print up?

---

c. How much money did the king borrow?

---

d. How much did the king's assets purchased with $1,000,000 increase in value? Why?

---

e. For those who lent money to the king, how much did they lose in value on the IOU? How much were they given in interest in the first year? What percentage did they lose on their investment in the first year (in total)?

---

32. By 2021, what percent of American families were on welfare (receiving government handouts)? What percent of Americans were on welfare (in total)?

33. Why is it harder to counterfeit a gold piece than paper money?

LIFE INTEGRATION AND SPIRITUAL APPLICATION

1. Read over Leviticus 19:35-37. Suppose you were selling hand-made soap or lemonade to customers. How might you make sure that it was an honest exchange?

2. Study Psalm 144:9–15, and answer the following questions.

a. Who does David want to be delivered from?

b. What does an honest society look like, according to the next verses?

c. How could our business and church communities treat each other with more honesty?

3. Consider 1 Timothy 6:10, and answer the following questions.

a. What is the root of all kinds of evil?

b. What are the roots of the breakdown of the US economy and the world economy?

8 INVESTMENTS - DON'T BURY YOUR TALENTS IN THE GROUND!

VOCABULARY AND TERMS

The following words or terms appear in the reading. Look up the definitions for each word in the glossary or in a dictionary. Match the word with the correct definition provided below.

________ 1. Consumables	a. an insurance intended to protect a client's property in case it is damaged during maintenance or servicing
________ 2. Capital Investment	b. monetary benefits to public workers when they retire
________ 3. Operating Expenses	c. revenue received for goods or services, or from other sources, as rents or investments
________ 4. Bonding	d. any property owned by a person or firm
________ 5. Broker	e. the amount of money invested or required to be invested in an enterprise or undertaking
________ 6. Options Market	f. a particular market where stocks and bonds are traded; stock exchange
________ 7. Stock Market	g. a savings plan that offers tax advantages to an individual depositor to set aside money for retirement
________ 8. Tithe	h. a profit arrived at by subtracting the cost of goods sold from gross revenue

_______ 9. Public Pension	i. a trading market wherein buyers are allowed the right to buy or sell a stock (or asset) at a stated price within a specified period
_______ 10. Tax break	j. a special tax benefit given to promote specific economic or social objectives
_______ 11. Individualized Retirement Account	k. an agent who buys or sells for a principal on a commission basis without having title to the property
_______ 12. Accounting	l. a total cost of the amount needed to operate and start up a business. An expense a business incurs through its normal business operations
_______ 13. Income	m. something that is produced to be consumed, such as processed food or fuel
_______ 14. Expenses	n. the skill, system, or job of keeping the financial records of a business or person
_______ 15. Net Revenue	o. an agreement in which the depositor allows the bank to retain the money deposited for a certain length of time
_______ 16. Assets	p. money paid out for charges or things purchased
_______ 17. Liabilities	q. money or compensation provided to an investor or bank depositor for the use of money deposited or loaned out
_______ 18. Depreciation	r. the tenth part of any thing; but appropriately, the tenth part of the increase and income arising from the profits of land and stock, to be given back to God to show our gratitude toward His abundant blessings
_______ 19. Interest	s. a decrease in the purchasing or exchange value of money
_______ 20. Certificate of Deposit	t. money owed or yet to be paid

STUDY QUESTIONS

1. Over a period of twenty years, one mama cow and her daughter cows might produce sixty cows (four generations). Suppose you owned three mama cows. How many cows might they produce in twenty years?

2. Given the example of how you might use $3,000 given in the book, answer the following questions.

   a. How much money was spent for bubble gum?

   b. How much money was spent on expensive tennis shoes?

   c. How much money was spent on capital investment?

   d. How much money was spent on operating expenses?

   e. How much money did the lemonade stand earn for you?

f. How much money did the bubble gum earn for you?

____

g. How much money did the tennis shoes earn for you?

____

h. What is your net worth after selling 500 cups of lemonade?

____

____

3. Consider the savings chart under the heading "Bank Savings, Bank Checking, and CD Accounts." Answer the following questions:

a. How much money did the saver make after 20 years, with 6% interest and 3% inflation? How much money did the saver appear to make?

____

____

b. How much money did the saver lose after 20 years, with 1% interest and 3% inflation? How much did the saver appear to make?

____

____

4. Consider the example of the young man who dedicated 20 hours to working at a sandwich shop for 10 years.

a. How many waking hours did he have left in a week after dedicating 20 hours to working at the sandwich shop?

b. How much money would he have saved if he was really able to get 6% interest on his savings?

c. What could the young man do with the other 82 waking hours of his week, (from ages 16 to 26)?

d. Why can't young men pay off a home at 26 years of age?

5. Why are government bonds a safe investment?

6. Why are government bonds a bad investment (at times)?

7. Why would you charge a higher interest when lending money to an irresponsible person?

8. Match the following stock exchanges to the description that best fits:

a. Standard and Poor Index	1) Averages America's most popular stock values
b. Nasdaq Index	2) Averages 500 largest companies stock values
c. Dow Jones Industrial Average	3) Averages tech company stock values

9. What are the two ways in which investors make money in the stock market?

10. What is a legitimate reason to invest in the stock market? What is the motivation of day traders who buy and sell stocks as quickly as they can?

11. What are some indications that a company is worth your investment? List several points contained in the text. Include some of your own ideas.

12. Suppose a trader buys a call option for 200 shares of ABC company's stock at $35. The stock is currently worth $25. He paid $200 for the option to purchase the stock at $35. The stock rises to $45. He exercises the option. Now, how much money did he make?

13. How did the US stock market turn into a casino in 2021? Which stock was most popular in the options market (or the gambling market)?

14. Why is the Price to Earnings ratio considered "the greed ratio"?

15. How long did it take for the markets to correct after the 2008 crash?

16. What is your best investment? What is your very best investment?

17. In the parable of the Rich Man and Lazarus, what was it that the Rich Man had failed to do?

18. How can you use real estate as an investment to provide a profit for you?

19. What are the challenges presented with real estate investments?

20. Name three of the best places in the US to own rental property in 2021. Name three of the worst places.

21. Why would it be wrong to refer to purchasing gold and silver as an investment?

22. Suppose you bought a house for $100,000, put a $10,000 down payment on the place, and took on a mortgage of $90,000. If the house price inflated $20,000 in three years (and you sold it for $120,000), how much money did you make?
What is your return on your investment?
If the house deflated, and you had to sell it for $80,000 in three years, how much money did you lose?
How much money would you owe the bank?

23. What is the best way to avoid debt?

24. Which nations in the world have the lowest savings rates?

25. If a reliable car costs $6,000, and you could save $300 per month; how many months would it take you to save up for the car?

26. What was the character trait demonstrated by the tortoise, and absent with the hare in the fable?

27. If you earn $500 in a month, how much does the US government take from your company and your paycheck for Social Security and Medicare taxes?

28. What is the basic biblical principle that undergirds principles of good accounting?

29. How is the IRA and the 401(k) a preferred way to save?

30. Assume that the government will not provide any social security aid for you in your later years (between the ages of 70 and 90). Assuming you will have only savings to keep you going, how much money will you have to save (if you could live on $24,000 per year).

LIFE INTEGRATION AND SPIRITUAL APPLICATION

1. Review Proverbs 27:23-27 once more. What are your flocks and herds? What are the things God has given you to take care of? How might you best take care of them?

2. What does spiritual growth and productivity look like in your life? What are the areas in which you could grow spiritually?

3. What are the two dangerous heart dispositions that surround investing in stocks? How might you avoid these heart attitudes? What is the Christian heart disposition that is just the opposite of these bad dispositions?

4. What are the three charitable requirements contained in the Old Testament? Reference Leviticus 19:9-10 for the third charitable requirement. Would you give more or less than this?

5. Review Luke 10:29-37.

a. What is the lesson the Lord teaches us with the Good Samaritan parable?

b. Who is our neighbor, as described in the parable?

c. Provide an example of some need that presented itself to you in the last six months. How did you respond?

6. Read Proverbs 13:22, Matthew 15:5-6, and 1 Timothy 5:4–8. What does God urge upon us in these passages? How does this differ from the world's systems today?

9 SEEKING GOOD GOVERNMENT - HOW GOVERNMENTS RUIN ECONOMIES

VOCABULARY AND TERMS

The following words or terms appear in the reading. Look up the definitions for each word in the glossary or in a dictionary. Match the word with the correct definition provided below.

_______ 1. Bribery

_______ 2. Pharmaceuticals

_______ 3. Subsidy

_______ 4. World Gross Product

_______ 5. Taxation

_______ 6. Excise Tax

a. the combined gross national income of all the countries in the world

b. government by the people; a government in which the people vote for their leaders

c. trade based on the unrestricted international exchange of goods with tariffs used only as a source of revenue

d. a sum of money demanded by a government for its support or for specific facilities or services, levied upon incomes, property, sales, etc.

e. a theory or system of social organization that advocates the ownership and control of the means of production and distribution, capital, land, etc., by the community as a whole, usually through a centralized government

f. a direct monetary aid furnished by a government to a private business, a charity organization, or the like

_______ 7. Socialism	g. government characterized by specialization of functions, adherence to fixed rules, and a hierarchy of authority
_______ 8. Democracy	h. the amount by which a sum of money falls short of the required amount
_______ 9. Bureaucracy	i. the state of poverty; the process of becoming poor
_______ 10. Impoverishment	j. a rule or order issued by an executive authority or the regulatory agency of a government and having the force of law
_______ 11. Free Trade	k. businesses that make medicinal drugs
_______ 12. Deficit	l. a tax on certain things that are made, sold, or used within a country
_______ 13. Tariff	m. a tax required for goods imported or exported
_______ 14. Regulations	n. an act of giving or taking a favor or money, promised in order to influence the judgment or conduct of a person in a position of trust (often government officials)

STUDY QUESTIONS

1. What is the best thing governments can do to help the free market economy?

____

____

____

2. What is the purpose for government as defined by Romans 13?

3. What percent of the US federal government's expenses are outside of God's assignments for government?

4. What are the five most corrupt nations in the world, and what is the primary religion or worldview of those nations?

5. What are the five most honest nations in the world, and what is the primary religion or worldview of those nations?

6. Take a look at the graph displaying campaign donations for the US Presidential race. In what year did these campaign donations (and dishonesty in American politics) start to increase very significantly?

7. Which company had the largest amount of campaign donations associated with it in the 2020 elections and received the most money in military contracts?

8. How much money did Pfizer and Moderna collect in government-mandated Covid-19 shots in 2020? How much money did the pharmaceuticals put into campaign donations? What was the ratio?

9. Based on the textbook summary, how much did government regulation and the percentage of government employees increase from 1933 to 2020?

10. What are rent controls?

11. How did the Covid-19 lockdowns affect the world's economy?

12. When and where did the localized tyranny of zoning and planning commissions begin?

13. Consider the chart of total hours spent by US adults in 2015. If the average person works for $25 per hour, how much money is wasted on filling out government paperwork?

____

____

____

14. Reference the US Government Revenue (1790-2015). Where were the three largest increases in government taxation in US history? Which presidents were involved?

____

____

____

____

15. 15. Suppose somebody earns $100,000 per year. If the graduated income tax rates are: 10% for the first $20,000, and 12% for everything he earns between $20,000 and $80,000, and 22% for everything over $80,000, how much income tax will that person have to pay?

10% x $20,000 = ______________

12% x $60,000 = ______________

22% x $20,000 = ______________

Total tax = ______________

16. Which of the following states do NOT have the following forms of taxation or maintain the lowest property tax rates? (Some research is required for this.) Which state would be the most favorable in your estimation.

State	Sales Tax (Mark None)	Property Tax (Mark Lowest)	Income Tax (Mark None
Wyoming			
Washington			
Texas			
Alaska			
Oregon			
New Hampshire			
Montana			
Louisiana			
Alabama			

17. Reference the table "How Much Did Governments Take from the People's Income?"

a. By what factor is the present US government expenditures/taxation greater than the Roman taxation during the time of Christ?

___

___

___

b. How much larger was the US government in 2020 vs. 1780?

______

______

______

______

18. What are the four basic biblical principles relating to taxation that should be incorporated into our governments?

a. ______

b. ______

c. ______

d. ______

19. a. What is the average GDP per capita (person) for the five most free nations in the world? (For the average, add up the five GDP per capita numbers, and divide by five.)

______

______

______

______

b. What is the average GDP per capita (person) for the five most enslaved tyrannical nations in the world?

____

____

____

____

c. What is the difference between these two averages? (Divide the little number by the big number, and you will get the factor indicating the difference.)

____

____

d. If you were looking for a country to settle down in, and you were concerned about freedom and prosperity, where would you go. . .

In Asia __________

In Western Europe ___________

In Northern Europe __________

In Eastern Europe __________

In North America __________

In South America __________

In Oceania __________

20. When did world freedoms start to disappear (in recent years)?

21. What is the purpose of the World Bank? What is the real purpose of handing out this money on the part of powerful governments?

22. List at least two ways governments should legitimately intervene in the free market economy.

23. What were the most dishonest nations in the world when it came to returning wallets? Which were the most honest countries?

LIFE INTEGRATION AND SPIRITUAL APPLICATION

1. Consider Deuteronomy 22:8 and Exodus 21:28-29.

a. What is the civil penalty for somebody who just lets his bull gore people, and then finally somebody dies of the goring? (Gross Negligence cases).

b. Does God's law provide for a government regulator who goes from farm to farm identifying bulls that are not restrained?

c. How many cases a year involve the death of somebody as a result of gross negligence in the business world (in the US)?

d. How much do government agencies collect in fines each year?

e. Look around your house, your storage sheds, and yard. Are there any rakes laying on the ground? Do you see anything potentially dangerous? What sorts of things can you take care of now to prevent accidents? If you do these things yourself (in accordance with God's law), you do not need government to regulate you.

2. Read over Nehemiah 5:3-6 and 1 Samuel 8:15-18.

a. What constitutes a tyranny according to these passages?

b. By how much does federal taxation exceed the biblical limit set in 1 Samuel 8:15?

c. What can we do to address this very serious rise in tyranny? Reference 1 Samuel 8:18.

3. Consider Deuteronomy 20:1-4. What would you do if you saw your neighbor's wallet lying on a park bench? Have you ever returned something belonging to somebody else?

4. What are some good ways you can be looking out for and preserving your neighbor's property?

HOW TO BE SUCCESSFUL IN BUSINESS 10

VOCABULARY AND TERMS

The following words or terms appear in the reading. Look up the definitions for each word in the glossary or in a dictionary. Match the word with the correct definition provided below.

________ 1. Needs	a. to be slow or late about doing something that should be done: to delay doing something until a later time because you do not want to do it or because you are lazy
________ 2. Desires	b. an inclination to put the most favorable construction upon actions and events or to anticipate the best possible outcome
________ 3. Trepidation	c. the totality of features and characteristics of a product or service that bear on its ability to satisfy a customer's needs or expectations; the degree of excellence produced
________ 4. Procrastination	d. a method used in business for achieving the highest levels of quality in production with minimal variation
________ 5. Optimism	e. a market condition where there are few sellers which can greatly influence price and other market factors
________ 6. Quality	f. a nervous or fearful feeling of uncertain agitation

________ 7. Accuracy	g. a measure of precision or dispersion, computed by taking the arithmetic mean of the absolute values of the deviations of the functional values from some central value, usually the mean or median
________ 8. Precision	h. exclusive control of a commodity or service in a particular market, or a control that makes possible the manipulation of price
________ 9. Average Deviation	i. a condition marked by the lack of something requisite, something essential for life like food and clothing
________ 10. 6-Sigma	j. the degree of correctness of a quantity
________ 11. Monopoly	k. the mere wish of a person to have a particular commodity
________ 12. Oligopoly	l. the degree of refinement with which an operation is performed or a measurement stated
________ 13. Average	m. monetary gain resulting from the employment of capital in any transaction, the difference between the amount spent and the amount earned
________ 14. Profit	n. the central value in a set, a measurement of accuracy

STUDY QUESTIONS

1. Identify 2-3 principles taught by "success gurus" that basically represent these biblical principles: "Love your neighbor as yourself" (Lev. 19:18) and "Whatever you want men to do to you, do also to them, for this is the Law and the Prophets" (Matt. 7:12).

2. What is absent in this wisdom provided by "worldly wise people"?

3. What is the difference between flattery and affirmation presented in Scripture, as opposed to Dale Carnegie's wisdom?

4. What is the difference between the confidence of the unbeliever and the confidence of the believer when it comes to work?

____

____

____

____

5. What verses in the Bible present the sowing and reaping principle?

____

____

____

6. Match the following verses with the principle the Bible enjoins for your life.
Verses: Luke 10:38–42, Proverbs 11:24–25, Proverbs 13:4, Proverbs 13:18, Proverbs 20:4, Ecclesiastes 9:10

a. Don't procrastinate

b. Use your resources. Don't be a miser.

c. Be diligent

d. Work in spite of obstacles.

e. Prioritize the important things in life.

f. Listen to correction.

7. What is the first mark of success in the Christian life?

8. Joseph was trustworthy. What were the four situations in which Joseph proved himself to be trustworthy?

9. What are the two positive characteristics demonstrated by Joseph in his work?

10. How was being honest a painful experience for Joseph?

11. What did Fundbox learn about the effects of dishonesty when companies are not quick to pay their invoices?

12. Give examples of how business people might lie about their competitors?

13. In your own words, explain how a godly salesman would operate. The text gave three basic principles.

a.

b.

c.

14. Why was the Christian-owned company Chick-fil-A so successful?

15. What was L.L. Bean's philosophy that produced such success for that company?

16. How does the text define quality in positive terms and negative terms?

17. What is the quality goal for high volume manufacturing and fast food restaurant chains?

18. Examine the following charts and determine whether accuracy is high or low, and whether precision is high or low for each chart.

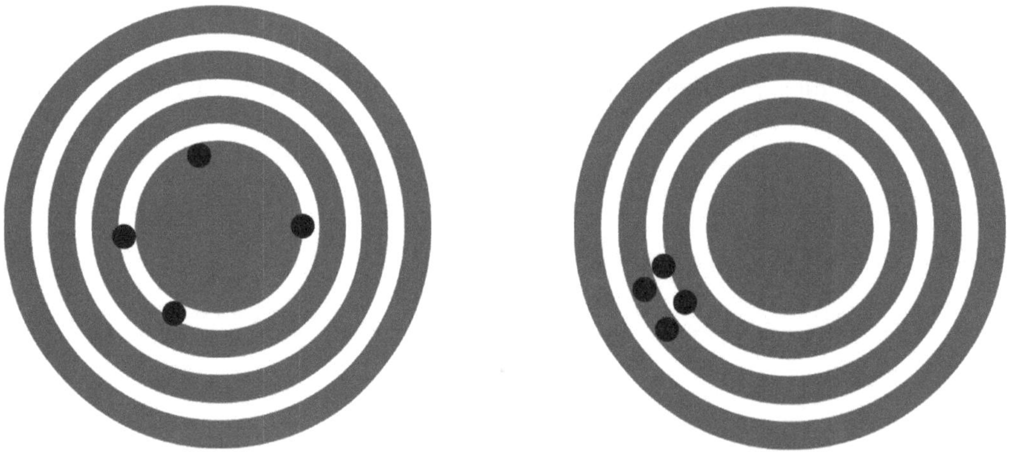

	Machine 1	Machine 2	Machine 3
	9.44	9.52	9.45
	9.44	9.51	9.45
	9.45	9.48	9.46
	9.46	9.43	9.46
	9.46	9.42	9.48
	9.51	9.47	9.50
	9.52	9.48	9.50
	9.44	9.49	9.47
	9.48	9.51	9.47
	9.52	9.47	9.50
Average (Mean)			
Target	9.47 inches	9.47 inches	9.47 inches
How many bad balls?			
Average deviation			

19. The NBA's official tolerance for the diameter of a basketball is 9.43 inches (24 cm) on the small side to 9.51 inches (24.16 cm) on the big side. The target is halfway between 9.43 and 9.51 inches, which would be 9.47 inches. Suppose you are working for a basketball manufacturer. Inspectors have measured the diameters of 10 balls coming out of the machine. Analyze the three machines making basketballs.

a. Calculate the averages for each. To get the average (mean), add the ten numbers in the column and divide by ten.
b. Calculate the average deviation for each. To get the average deviation, add up each deviation from the target, and divide by 10.
c. Which machine came closest to the target (on the average or mean)?
d. Which machine had the smallest deviation?
e. Which machine had the fewest bad balls? Which was the best machine for producing basketballs?

LIFE INTEGRATION AND SPIRITUAL APPLICATION

1. Consider Proverbs 24:3-4. What is wisdom, as best as you can describe it using biblical terms?

2. Read Proverbs 22:4. From the wisdom conveyed in this verse, answer the following questions. Do you think a person would be successful if he/she just read 1,000 business success books provided by the world? What is the secret to success according to this verse?

3. Consider the wisdom Dr. Thomas Stanley gleaned from millionaires in America. What Bible verses can you find that substantiate these values?
   a. Telling the truth

b. Hard work

c. Self-discipline

d. Getting along with others

e. Teaming up with a supportive spouse

4. Read Mark 11:22-24. How does your trust in God help you in your school work and other work? How often do you pray about your work? How often do you ask God for extra ability to perform your tasks? Have you experienced breakthroughs that come by faith in your work?

5. What is the "Biblical Secret to Success in Life" as presented in the 5th commandment? How are you growing in this area?

6. Review the section on procrastination. What are some of the corrections you could make in your life to avoid the habit of procrastination?

7. Plan out your day tomorrow (or next week) using the Franklin-Covey approach.

First, list out some of your goals for this year.
Then, list out the things you have to do and mark them either "Yes" or "No" for urgent and important.

Finally, prioritize the things you have to do, with an A, B, or C.

Urgent: Requires immediate action
Important: Important or significant for the fulfillment of your goals.

My Goals for This Year:

1.

2.

3.

Priority	Things to Do	Urgent	Important

11 MAKING WISE PURCHASING CHOICES

STUDY QUESTIONS

1. What are the two ways to save more money?

2. What are the biggest ticket items in a US household budget?

3. If a bike with an aluminum frame lasts for ten years (and costs $100), and a bike with a carbon or titanium frame lasts about forty years, how much would you pay for a bike with the more expensive frame?

4. What are the two most durable passenger vehicles according to the chart in the book?

5. What are the two most durable used passenger cars?

6. Examine the 10 year depreciation chart. How much does the Ford Escape depreciate in the first year? In order to take advantage of the most value for the most economical price, at what point in a Ford Escape automobile's life would you want to make the purchase?

7. Take a look at the chart featuring Best and Worst New Cars for Depreciation. What is the best car on the list for lowest depreciation in 5 years? What is the worst car on the list for depreciation?

8. Take a look at the chart featuring the Fiesta, Camry, and Accent. Which vehicle would require the lowest costs per year? Why?

9. When purchasing a used car, how can you find out if the vehicle had been in an accident?

10. What are your biggest expenses when you are just starting out in life?

11. How much might Christians save using Christian Medical Sharing instead of using regular insurance?

12. On average, how much could you save in a year if you did your own car maintenance?

13. What is the most important safety requirement before working on appliances?

14. What is your biggest energy cost in the home?

15. What are "deal killers" when buying a home? Give several examples.

16. How much could you save in a month, or in a year if. . .

a. You limited your phone/online access to 4 GB per month over the average of $114 per month?

b. You kept the thermostat at 64 F, instead of at 70 F during the winter months of November until March?

c. You did all your own basic maintenance on your car?

d. You used Christian Medical Sharing instead of typical health insurance (for a single person)?

e. You drive a Honda Civic at 36 mpg instead of a Ford Mustang at 26 mpg, for 14,263 miles per year (at an average of $4.00 per gallon)?

f. You avoid buying a coffee/espresso twice a week at $4.00 per cup.

17. Add up the savings in #16, and determine how much you save in ten years on these.

LIFE INTEGRATION AND SPIRITUAL APPLICATION

1. Young women: What are the qualities that Proverbs 31 extol?
   Young men: What are the qualities that 1 Timothy 5:8 extol?

2. Research the purchase of an automobile in your area. Consider three different models based upon your best guess on reliability. What can you get for $4,000 - $6,000? Be sure that the automobile has less than 150,000 miles on it. Use the Average Maintenance Cost in the text as your guide to calculate the amount of money needed for maintenance per year. Under teacher/parent oversight, complete a chart similar to the Fiesta/Camry/Accent chart in the text.

	Model 1:	Model 2 :	Model 3:
Price			
Average Maintenance Cost			
Miles per Gallon			
Gas (90,000 miles)			
Total Cost for 6 Years			
Average Cost per Year			

3. Of the seven suggestions for handling a home purchase "if you are poor," which do you find most helpful?

____

____

____

4. Pretend you are starting out as a family of two, and you need to develop your first budget. With parent/teacher oversight, research rentals, insurance costs, utility costs, etc. to find your best values. Fill in the blanks in the following chart:

Item	Household Budget (US)	Your Budget
Housing	$1,674	
Transportation	$813	
Auto Insurance	$120.00	
Healthcare	$414	
Groceries	$372	
Restaurants and other meals on the road	$288	
Entertainment	$269	
Utilities	$169	
Charity/Tithe	$157	
Apparel and services	$156	
Education	$117	
Personal care	$64	
SAVINGS	$500.00	
TOTAL SPENDING	$5513.00	

12 HOW BUSINESSES RUN

VOCABULARY AND TERMS

The following words or terms appear in the reading. Look up the definitions for each word in the glossary or in a dictionary. Match the word with the correct definition provided below.

________ 1. Contract	a. uncritical satisfaction with oneself, especially when accompanied by unawareness of actual dangers or deficiencies
________ 2. Covenantal Organization	b. the total cost needed to bring a project to a commercially operable status
________ 3. Risk	c. a legal claim of one person upon the property of another person to secure the payment of a debt or the satisfaction of an obligation
________ 4. Entrepreneurship	d. in business, the probability that an investment will lose value
________ 5. Proprietorship	e. a business arrangement for the supply of goods or services at a fixed price
________ 6. Complacency	f. owning a business establishment, or having the exclusive right or title to something; an owner, as of real property

_______ 7. Market Analysis	g. an expense used for covering a client's property in case it is damaged while performing a maintenance, or servicing
_______ 8. Demographics	h. a phase of marketing research conducted to determine the characteristics and extent of a market. The process of determining factors, conditions, and characteristics of a market
_______ 9. Capital Costs	i. organizing and managing any enterprise, especially a business, usually with considerable initiative and risk
_______ 10. Bonding	j. a specific segment of a group of people having shared characteristics
_______ 11.Lien	k. a collection of persons organized by contract or covenant, but maintained by nurturing the relationship. Family and church relationships are in this category

STUDY QUESTIONS

1. When you buy something in the marketplace, you receive a contract. What is this called?

____

____

____

2. What percentage of businesses survive five years (in the US)?

3. List the five reasons why businesses don’t make it, using your own words.

4. Which kind of demographic would be more likely to offer business to a lawn care enterprise — poor immigrant families or retired middle class/upper class older people? Why?

5. What kind of product or service would . . .
   a. Women be more likely to use?

   b. Children be more likely to use?

   c. Men be more likely to use?

   d. Older people be more likely to use?

6. If there are only 200 homes in your neighborhood and ten lawn care businesses, how many lawns might each business get? If there are 2,000 homes in your neighborhood and two lawn care companies, how many lawns might each business get?

7. Given the following business concepts and demographics described, how much income could you potentially get per week (if you started up the business, and God blessed your business)?

a. You start up a lemonade business in a street corner where 250 cars pass per day. You sell your lemonade for $3.00 for 6 days a week. (The average number of occupants in the car is 1.4.)

b. You start up an espresso machine on a street corner, where 100 cars pass by per day (in the morning hours). 64% of Americans drink coffee, and you sell your espressos/lattes for $4.00.

c. You start up a lawn care business in a neighborhood largely populated by middle-income elderly, retired people. There are 200 yards in the area, and you will charge $120 per month for yard maintenance.

8. What is the best way to determine market needs?

9. What are examples of barriers to entry for businesses?

10. What are ways in which you would have to pay your dues, if you are starting up a new business?

11. If your business is inconsistent (slow sometimes and busy at other times), what should you do in terms of hiring employees?

12. If the business runs out of money, how should a Christian manager pay his employees?

13. What is the contract between the Employer and Employee called?

14. List the five reasons why businesses don't make it, using your own words.

15. Which kind of demographic would be more likely to offer business to a lawn care enterprise— poor immigrant families or retired middle class/upper class older people? Why?

16. What is the worst problem faced by businesses (in relation to their employees)?

17. What defines a Christian culture in businesses?

18. What are the five things employees desire out of their employment?

19. What are the three questions that should be asked before saying anything?

20. How do good managers lead as Jesus led?

LIFE INTEGRATION AND SPIRITUAL APPLICATION

1. Study 1 Corinthians 13 and make a comment on how the following qualities should affect your speech in business relationships.

   a. Love is not rude.

   b. Love is patient

   c. Love is kind.

d. Love is not easily provoked.

e. Love bears all things.

2. How is a Christian to address the Monday morning challenge? What is your attitude on Monday mornings?

3. Read over Proverbs 27:6 and Proverbs 28:23 once more. How do you respond to criticism and correction from Dad and Mom, or from your managers? Will you be successful in life?

4. Consider the section: "How to Grow Yourself to Be a Better Employee and Professional." Are you a good worker? Would you hire yourself for a job?

What are your weaknesses? What are your sinful tendencies that get in the way of your communication with others?

In this section of the text, what have you learned to help you in these areas?

5. Consider the various types of labor outlined in this chapter. Business owners. Managers. Sales. Technicians. Creators and Engineers. Accountants. Inspectors. How will you fit into the world economy? What are your talents and what can you say about God's calling on your life right now?

YOUR CALLING IN LIFE 13

VOCABULARY AND TERMS

The following words or terms appear in the reading. Look up the definitions for each word in the glossary or in a dictionary. Match the word with the correct definition provided below.

________ 1. Aptitude	a. something that is given to you or done for you in return for something you have given to or done for someone else
________ 2. Quid-pro-quo	b. adequate; possession of sufficient knowledge, skill, qualification, or capacity
________ 3. Aggregate	c. the position or services under a wise and trusted counselor or senior sponsor, often including life integration and hands-on experience in a particular field
________ 4. Competency	d. capability; ability; innate or acquired capacity for something; talent
________ 5. Mentorship	e. a sum, mass, or assemblage of particulars; a total or gross amount

STUDY QUESTIONS

1. Why can we say that a man drafted into military service is called to it? How does this relate to our life's calling?

2. Why is the phrase, "If you can dream it, you can do it," wrong? Compare with James 4:13-16.

3. How does the text describe God's calling on your life?

4. What are the sorts of things that your life's calling includes?

5. If you are faced with three opportunities at one time, which do you choose?

6. What are the two "wills" of God? Which can we learn more about?

7. If we are to seek the kingdom of God first, what does this consist of? Explain each of these three elements in your own words.

a.

b.

c.

8. If men have 26 pounds (12 kg) more muscle mass than women, and women have 40 percent less upper-body strength on average, how might this itself put men in different work than women?

9. What are the basic work skills every young person should learn (in relation to the work world)?

10. What are some of the college alternatives that may turn out to be more cost and time effective for the average student?

11. For what purposes were colleges built at the beginning of this country (the US)? How did that change?

12. How much did college debt increase in the US (as a percentage of the GDP)?

13. How long would it take for the average college graduate to pay off his debt (as compared to the average college graduate in 1975)?

14. What are the college majors with the best return on investment? What are the worst?

15. Why is Switzerland's unemployment at 2% while other nations were upwards of 20-30% in recent surveys?

LIFE INTEGRATION AND SPIRITUAL APPLICATION

1. Assess where you are right now and how this ties into God's calling on your life.

   a. What opportunities has God brought to your door?

   b. What has God already enabled you to accomplish in your life (in the work world)?

c. What gifts and abilities has God given to you?

d. What finances has He provided for your education?

e. What family background gives you some entrance to the economy?

f. How does all this relate to God's calling on your life?

2. Consider your gifts against the following list of aptitudes used in the workplace. Rate yourself from 1 to 10 on each.

Aptitude	Rating
Inductive Reasoning Aptitude	
Auditory Aptitude	
Physical Aptitude	
Linguistic Aptitude	
Numerical Aptitude	
Clerical Aptitude	
Analytical Aptitude	
Mechanical Aptitude	
Artistic Aptitude	

3. What biblical principle is God enjoining for men in these verses?

a. Genesis 3:17-19

b. 1 Timothy 5:5-8

c. Nehemiah 4:14

d. Ephesians 5:25-28

e. Ephesians 6:4

f. If you are a young man, how are you preparing for these roles and responsibilities?

4. What biblical principle is God enjoining for women in these verses?

a. Genesis 2:18-22

b. 1 Timothy 5:14

c. 1 Timothy 2:9-15

d. If you are a young woman, how are you preparing for these roles and responsibilities?

5. Consider Proverbs 13:20. How does one achieve wisdom? How have you applied this in your life? How do you intend to apply this for the next three years?

6. What are the three "legs on the stool" for preparing yourself for your life's calling? How are you best providing for these elements in your preparation for life?

FINAL EXAM

TOTAL POINTS: 40

VOCABULARY AND TERMS

The following words or terms appear in the reading. Look up the definitions for each word in the glossary or in a dictionary. Match the word with the correct definition provided below.

________ 1. Supply	a. a legal entity formed by a group of one or more investors
________ 2. Investment	b. a social system that existed in Europe during the Middle Ages in which people worked and fought for nobles who gave them protection and the use of land in return
________ 3. Scarcity	c. the tenth part of any thing; but appropriately, the tenth part of the increase and income arising from the profits of land and stock, to be given back to God to show our gratitude toward His abundant blessings
________ 4. Trade	d. a system of social organization in which all economic and social activity is controlled by a totalitarian state dominated by a single and self-perpetuating political party
________ 5. Macroeconomy	e. an insurance intended to protect a client's property in case it is damaged during maintenance or servicing
________ 6. Corporation	f. a savings plan that offers tax advantages to an individual depositor to set aside money for retirement

________ 7. Communism	g. a tax required for goods imported or exported
________ 8. Feudalism	h. insufficiency or shortness of supply; dearth
________ 9. Family Economy	i. a quantity of something on hand or available, as for use; a stock or store
________ 10. Tithe	j. all the work, all the buying and selling, and all the useful things made by a whole nation of people working together
________ 11. Bonding	k. the skill, system, or job of keeping the financial records of a business or person
________ 12. Accounting	l. any property owned by a person or firm
________ 13. Individualized Retirement Account	m. an act of giving or taking money or favor, promised in order to influence the judgment or conduct of a person in a position of trust (often government officials)
________ 14. Assets	n. the totality of features and characteristics of a product or service that bear on its ability to satisfy a customer's needs or expectations; the degree of excellence produced
________ 15. Tariffs	o. the act or process of buying, selling, or exchanging commodities, at either wholesale or retail, within a country or between countries
________ 16. Bribery	p. God's original plan for economic stewardship of His creation where the family works together in reliance upon the Lord, each other, and other families in their community; they do not rely on governments and corporations
________ 17. Quality	q. the outlay of money usually for income or profit

SHORT ANSWER

1. The root of all kinds of evil (according to 1 Timothy 6:10) is ______________________.

2. Jesus said, "You cannot serve God and ____________________."

3. __________________ calls for the abolition of private property.

4. The year of _____________________ was the year the Israelites set the captives/slaves free.

5. The wicked borrow and do not __________________.

6. Whatsoever a man sows, that shall he also ______________.

LONGER ANSWER:

1. Name at least two inventions that provided for significant division of labor in the modern world.

____

____

____

____

2. What was the primary cause of famines in the twentieth century?

____

____

____

____

3. List at least 3 requirements for money.

4. What were two ways that deceitful people reduced the value of silver and gold in past history?

5. What is a "run on the bank"?

6. What is the organization called that controls the value of money in the US economy?

---

7. Who is helped the most when governments enact inflationary policies? Circle all that apply.

a. Poor widows

b. Rich governments

c. Debtors

d. Retirees

e. Students

8. What is the punishment required by God's law for somebody who is so negligent, he/she allows a life-threatening condition (like a bull that attacks people) to kill somebody?

---

9. What is the difference between the confidence of the unbeliever, and the confidence of the believer when it comes to work?

10. Joseph's honesty was not a result of the fact that his employers were watching him. Why did he maintain some honesty and moral integrity?

BASIC ACCOUNTING AND BUSINESS MATH

1. A lemonade business spent $50 on lemons, $20 on sugar, $50 hiring a friend to do the work, and $40 on plastic cups. The business sold 100 cups of lemonade at $4.00 a cup. How much profit did the business earn?

2. You put $1,000 into a bank account at 5% interest.
   a. How much interest do you earn in one year?

   b. If inflation is 4%, how much monetary value did you lose by inflation?

3. You have $1,000 in a savings account. You have $30 in your pocket. You have just built a lemonade stand using materials that cost about $2,000. What is your net worth (or the value of all your assets put together)?

4. You earned $2,000 in the last year. What should you offer to God in your tithes for the year?

5. The US receives $700 billion in imported goods from China. The US exports $150 billion in imported goods to China. What is the trade deficit?

6. A young man put $10,000 of his own money into a $100,000 house. He borrowed $90,000. Because of a downturn, he had to sell the house for $80,000 within a year. How much money did he lose? How much money does he have to pay the bank (assuming he didn't pay down the loan)?

7. Your annual expenses are $1,000 for car insurance, $600 for gas, $300 for car maintenance, $500 for food and entertainment, and $400 for church tithe and giving. What do you need for an annual income? What should your monthly income be?

THE BIG PROJECT

The big project is intended to tie together several important components.

1. Basic Mentorship
2. Work that Produces Economic Value
3. Character Development and Continuous Improvement
4. The Life-Integrated Experience (Learn By Doing)

This project should provide the student with an opportunity for personal growth in knowledge and character in relation to the work world.

MONTH #1 – TO BEGIN

At the beginning of the course, the student chooses one of the following five projects listed below. The decision should involve parents/teachers and prayer for God's Wisdom. By the end of the fourth week, the student should have laid out the plan and goals for the project.

1. Create and market a product.

2. Take on a more responsible role in a family business, or contribute something to the development of it.

3. Start your own business (lemonade stand or yard maintenance business, or. . .).

4. Interview for a job and work the job for eight months.

5. Volunteer for a position with a non-profit ministry or church.
   The first three selections would best fit a more entrepreneurial-minded young person. An honest assessment of oneself by the questions laid out in the text is important before choosing this option.

Are you a self-starter? Do you like to do things your own way? Are you self-motivated enough that you don't need anybody to tell you what to do each day?

Are you able to motivate others to follow you? Do people like to follow your ideas?

Are you the kind of person who likes to take charge? Do you want to make sure that the project gets completed? Or do you get discouraged and just walk away?

Can you keep going when the going gets tough? Are you a super- hard worker even when work is difficult? Will you make sure the job gets done no matter how hard it might be?

Can you make quick decisions with wise input from others?

Are you able to take risks and make mistakes without worrying too much about failure?

Are you careful not to get bogged down or distracted by unimportant things?

Are you able to handle a wide variety of tasks in the business?

Can you pay attention to a lot of different things at the same time without stressing out?

If the student cannot answer yes to most of these questions, it would be better to look for a job or a volunteer position with a non-profit organization.

IDENTIFY A BUSINESS MENTOR

Over the first 3-4 weeks, choose a business mentor. This could be a parent, or at least, be sure that your parents are involved in the decision. The mentor could be a supervisor or a manager in the business where you will work, or the ministry where you will volunteer. Meet with the mentor and be sure you have got an agreement that the mentor will answer your questions, provide valuable input, and assess your growth as a worker or businessman/woman. Ideally, your mentor has already proved to be successful in business of some kind.

We recommend that a woman mentor a young woman, and a man mentor a young man, but most importantly the mentor should be one trusted by your family.

HOW TO IDENTIFY A GOOD MENTOR

When you meet with a mentor, go prepared with 3-5 questions to ask. You are looking for a mentor who is:

- Experienced in the field you are working in, or just experienced in starting up or managing businesses

- Interested in your success

- Acts like a coach and wants to see your character and faith formed at the same time that you succeed in business

- Will dedicate a little time for you on a monthly or weekly basis

- Will challenge you as well as encourage you in what you are doing

GOALS

After choosing your project and before beginning the job or the work for this "Big Project," lay out the goals you would like to achieve over the next 8-9 months. Your mentor/teacher/parent should be able to help you with these goals. Use Worksheet Number One for these goals.

WORKSHEET #1

Personal Goals

I would like to improve my character, work habits, and faith in the following areas:

1.

2.

3.

Work Competencies

I would like to become more competent or learn more about business in the following areas:

1.

2.

3.

Success Goals

I would like to achieve these following goals in the specific job or work that I have set out to do:

1.

2.

3.

MONTHS 2 - 8

Ideally, you will need to spend 5-20 hours a week working on the project. This makes up the practical part of this course in life skills. At the end of the 3rd month, ask your employer/supervisor/mentor/teacher/parent to help you fill out the Third Month Evaluation Form - Worksheet #2.

At the end of the 6th month, ask your employer/supervisor/mentor/teacher/parent to help you fill out the Sixth Month Evaluation Form - Worksheet #3.

WORKSHEET #2

Third Month Evaluation Form

Name: ______________________________

Project: ______________________________

Date: ____________________

1. What progress has been made in achieving the student's personal goals?

____

____

____

____

2. What progress has been made in achieving the student's goals for work competencies?

____

____

____

3. What progress has been made in achieving the student's success goals?

4. How would you rate the quality of the student's work?

5. How has the student grown in the quality of work produced over the last 3 months?

6. How would you rate the quantity of the student's work?

7. How has the student grown in the quantity of work produced over the last 3 months?

8. How well does this student interact with others in the workplace? Specify for customers, fellow workers, and managers.

9. How well does the student follow through on advice given by counselors/mentors/employers?

10. What is the most important area of improvement needed right now for the student to succeed in this project over the next three months?

11. Has the student produced anything or sold anything that has added value to the market (or to the ministry)? How many people has the student blessed by this work? Or, how much income has the student produced for the company? Specify as best as possible.

____

____

____

____

____

____

12. What financial reward or other kind of reward should the student receive or has the student received as a result of his/her work?

____

____

____

____

____

WORKSHEET #3

Sixth Month Evaluation Form

Name: ______________________________________

Project:______________________________________

Date: ___________________________

1. What progress has been made in achieving the student's personal goals?

____

____

____

____

2. What progress has been made in achieving the student's goals for work competencies?

____

____

____

____

3. What progress has been made in achieving the student's success goals?

4. How would you rate the quality of the student's work?

5. How has the student grown in the quality of work produced over the last 3 months?

6. How would you rate the quantity of the student's work?

7. How has the student grown in the quantity of work produced over the last 3 months?

8. How well does this student interact with others in the workplace? Specify for customers, fellow workers, and managers.

9. How well does the student follow through on advice given by counselors/mentors/employers?

10. What is the most important area of improvement needed right now for the student to succeed in this project over the next three months?

11. Has the student produced anything or sold anything that has added value to the market (or to the ministry)? How many people has the student blessed by this work? Or, how much income has the student produced for the company? Specify as best as possible.

12. What financial reward or other kind of reward should the student receive or has the student received as a result of his/her work?

PROJECT COMPLETION

At the end of the 9th month, ask your employer/supervisor/mentor/teacher/parent to help you fill out the Final Assessment Form - Worksheet #4. This will constitute your score for the project.

WORKSHEET #4

Final Assessment Form

Name: ______________________________

Project:______________________________

Date: ______________________

Total Points: __________

Did the student contribute some helpful service or a value-add to the economy (or ministry)? Rate according to the following scoring:

___ A high level of value-add - 30 points

___ An average, moderate level of value-add - 25 points

___ A low level of value-add - 10 points

Did the student register improvement and work towards achieving the initial goals set down at the beginning of the project? Rate according to the following scoring:

___ Steady and significant progress - 30 points

___ Moderate progress - 25 points

___ A little progress - 15 points

___ No progress - 5 points

To what extent were the customers/managers satisfied with the work produced?

__Very satisfied - 30 points

__ Reasonably satisfied - 25 points

__ Minimally satisfied - 10 points

__ Not satisfied at all - 0 points

To what extent did the student follow through on orders and complete the job?

__ Completed the job to a high degree of satisfaction - 10 points

__ Completed the job - 8 points

__ Completed half the job - 5 points

__ Did not complete the job and did not follow through - 0 points

Would you hire this young person for your business?______________

Would you recommend this young person for another person's business? ______________

To what degree would you say this young person will succeed in the following areas? Rate at 1 (low) to 10 (high).

Entrepreneurship ______

Management _______

Apprenticeship _______

Trades _______

Employee ________

What is the most important area of personal growth needed if this student will achieve a high level of success in the business or ministry world?

What gifts/talents have you discerned about the student following this work experience?

GLOSSARY

6-Sigma - a method used in business for achieving the highest levels of quality in production with minimal variation

A

Accounting - the skill, system, or job of keeping the financial records of a business or person

Accuracy - the degree of correctness of a quantity

Aggregate - a sum, mass, or assemblage of particulars; a total or gross amount

Apprenticeship - a program or position in which someone learns a trade by working under a certified expert

Aptitude - capability; ability; innate or acquired capacity for something; talent

Arbiter - a person empowered to decide matters at issue; judge; umpire

Assets - any property owned by a person or firm

Average - the central value in a set, a measurement of accuracy

Average Deviation - a measure of dispersion, computed by taking the arithmetic mean of the absolute values of the deviations of the functional values from some central value, usually the mean or median

B

Bankruptcy - any insolvent debtor; a person unable to satisfy any just claims made upon him or her. In utter ruin, failure, depletion, or the like: utter impoverishment

Barter Economy - an economy where exchange of commodities are solely based upon trades rather than by the use of money

Bitcoin - a type of cryptocurrency popular in the 2020s

Bonding - an insurance intended to protect a client's property in case it is damaged during maintenance or servicing

Bribery - an act of giving or taking money or favor promised in order to influence the judgment or conduct of a person in a position of trust, often government officials

Broker - an agent who buys or sells for a principal on a commission basis without having title to the property

Bureaucracy - government characterized by specialization of functions, adherence to fixed rules, and a hierarchy of authority

C

Capital Costs - the total cost needed to bring a project to a commercially operable status

Capital Investment -	the amount of money invested or required to be invested in an enterprise or undertaking
Capitalism -	an economic system in which investment in and ownership of the means of production, distribution, and exchange of wealth is made and maintained chiefly by private individuals or corporations, especially as contrasted to cooperatively or state-owned means of wealth
Civil Government -	the practical implementation of a state on behalf of its citizens
Collectivism -	the political principle of centralized social and economic control, especially of all means of production
Common Grace -	God's indiscriminate kindness and mercy which preserve all men, believers and unbelievers, through the abundant and daily blessings of earthly life
Communism -	a system of social organization in which all economic and social activity is controlled by a totalitarian state dominated by a single and self-perpetuating political party
Communist Manifesto -	a pamphlet (1848) by Karl Marx and Friedrich Engels: first statement of the principles of modern communism
Competency -	adequate; possession of sufficient knowledge, skill, qualification, or capacity
Complacency -	self-satisfaction especially when accompanied by unawareness of actual dangers or deficiencies
Conscientiousness -	governed by conscience; controlled by or done according to one's inner sense of what is right; principled

Constituent - serving to compose or make up a thing; component

Consumables - something that is produced to be consumed, as processed food or fuel

Contract Labor - labor coercible by the enforceable provisions of a contract

Contracts - a business arrangement for the supply of goods or services at a fixed price

Corporation - a legal entity formed by a group of one or more investors

Counterfeit - made as an imitation so as to be passed off fraudulently or deceptively as genuine; forged

Covenantal Organization - an organization organized by contract or covenant, but maintained by nurturing the relationship. Families and Churches are in this category

Cryptocurrencies - any form of currency that only exists digitally, that usually has no central issuing or regulating authority but instead uses a decetralized system to record transactions and manage the issuance of new units, and that relies on cryptography to prevent counterfeiting and fraudulent transactions

D

Daring - venturesomely bold in action or thought

Debt - a state of being under obligation to pay or repay someone or something in return for something received: a state of servanthood or slavery

Decentralize - to distribute the administrative powers or functions of (a central authority) over a less concentrated area

Deficit - the amount by which a sum of money falls short of the required amount

Demand - the quantity of a commodity or service wanted at a specified price and time

Democracy - government by the people; a system of governance in which the people vote for their leaders

Demographics - a specific segment of a population having shared characteristics

Deposit - to place for safekeeping or in trust, especially in a bank account: to give as security or in part payment

Depreciation - a decrease in the purchasing or exchange value of money

Desires - the mere wish of a person to have a particular commodity

Despair - to lose all hope or confidence

Devoid - being without a usual, typical, or expected attribute or accompaniment

Distributism - the theory or practice of distributing private property (as land) to the maximum degree among individual owners

E

Economics - the study of how wealth or value is produced, consumed, and transferred

Economy - all the activity of a household, a community, or a country, etc., usually referring to the financial business of producing, buying, and selling; the management of this human activity

Efficiency - the ability to do something or produce something without wasting materials, time, or energy: the quality or degree of being efficient

Entrepreneurship - organizing and managing any enterprise, especially a business, usually with considerable initiative and risk

Entropy - the degradation or decay of matter and energy in the universe

Exchange Value - Value set on a product by the market

Excise Tax - a tax on certain things that are made, sold, or used within a country

Expenses - money paid out for charges or things purchased

F

Family Economy - God's original plan for economic stewardship of His creation where each member of the family contribute to their daily needs and rely upon the Lord, each other, and other families in their community. They do not rely on governments and corporations

Feudalism - a social system that existed in Europe during the Middle Ages in which people worked and fought for nobles who gave them protection and the use of land in return

Finance - the management of revenues; the conduct or transaction of money matters generally, especially those affecting the public, as in the fields of banking and investment

Fractional Reserve Banking - a practice in which banks will lend out more money than that which they hold in reserve

Franchise - a method of distributing products or services in which a party pays a fee and/or royalties to use a brand's trademark, trade name, and business approach

Free Trade - trade based on the unrestricted international exchange of goods with tariffs used only as a source of revenue

G

Gross Domestic Product (GDP) - the value of all the goods and services produced within a country (usually over a period of a year)

I

Impoverishment - the state of poverty; the process of becoming poor

Income - revenue received for goods or services, or from other sources, as rents or investments

Incompetent - lacking the qualities needed for effective action: inadequate to or unsuitable for a particular purpose

Indenture - a contract by which a person, as an apprentice, is bound to service

Individualism - a social theory advocating the liberty, rights, or independent action of the individual: the pursuit of individual rather than common or collective interests

Individualized Retirement Account - a savings plan that offers tax advantages to an individual depositor to set aside money for retirement

Inflation - a persistent, substantial rise in the general level of prices related to an increase in the volume of money and resulting in the loss of currency value

Interest - a sum paid or charged for the use of money or for borrowing money

Investment - the outlay of money usually for income or profit

J

Jubilee - a year of emancipation and restoration provided to be kept every 50 years by the emancipation of the enslaved, restoration of alienated lands to their former owners, and omission of all cultivation of the land

Judicious - having, exercising, or characterized by sound judgment

L

Labor - the services performed by workers for wages as distinguished from those rendered by entrepreneurs for profits

Liabilities - money owed and yet to be paid

Lien -	the legal claim of one person upon the property of another person to secure the payment of a debt or the satisfaction of an obligation
Life Integration -	basic principle for all of learning, where an individual applies, put into practice, and have a hands-on experience of the important principles he or she learned; especially in a family economy setting

M

M1 Money Supply -	the total of amount of money contained in US checking accounts, coins, and currencies
Macroeconomy -	all the work, all the buying and selling, and all the useful things made by a whole nation of people working together
Magna Carta -	the "great charter" of English liberties, forced from King John by the English barons and sealed at Runnymede, June 15, 1215: any fundamental constitution or law guaranteeing rights and liberties
Mammon -	material wealth or possessions especially as having a debasing influence
Manumission -	to release from slavery or servitude
Market -	the course of commercial activity by which the exchange of commodities is effected : extent of demand
Market Analysis -	a phase of marketing research conducted to determine the characteristics and extent of a market. The process of determining factors, conditions, and characteristics of a market

Materialism - preoccupation with or emphasis on material objects, comforts, and considerations, with a disinterest in or rejection of spiritual, intellectual, or cultural values

Mentorship - the position or services under a wise and trusted counselor or senior sponsor, often including life integration and hands-on experience in a particular field

Mercantilism - a government enforced monopoly to unify and increase the power and especially the monetary wealth of a nation by a strict governmental regulation of the entire national economy usually through policies designed to secure an accumulation of bullion

Microeconomy - one individual's or one household's participation in the economy

Miserliness - of, like, or befitting a person who lives in wretched circumstances in order to save and hoard money

Mixed Economies - an economy in which there are elements of both public and private enterprise

Monopoly - exclusive control of a commodity or service in a particular market, or a control that makes possible the manipulation of prices

Motivation - something such as a need or desire that causes a person to act

N

Needs - a condition marked by the lack of something requisite, something essential for life like food and clothing

Net Revenue -	a profit subtracting the cost of goods sold from gross revenue

O

Obsolete -	no longer used because something newer exists
Oligopoly -	a market condition where there are few sellers which can greatly influence price and other market factors
Operating Expenses -	a total cost of the amount needed to operate and start up a business. An expense a business incurs through its normal business operations
Optimism -	an inclination to put the most favorable construction upon actions and events or to anticipate the best possible outcome
Options Market -	a trading market wherein buyers are allowed the right to buy or sell a stock (or asset) at a stated price within a specified period

P

Partnership -	a legal relation existing between two or more persons contractually associated as joint principals in a business
Perceived Useful Value -	the customers' evaluation of the merits of a product or service
Perdition -	utter destruction or ruin
Pharmaceuticals -	businesses that make medicinal drugs

Precision - the degree of refinement with which an operation is performed or a measurement stated

Procrastination - to be slow or late about doing something that should be done: to delay doing something until a later time because you do not want to do it, because you are lazy, etc.

Profit - monetary gain resulting from the employment of capital in any transaction, the difference between the amount spent and the amount earned

Proprietorship - owning a business establishment, or having the exclusive right or title to something; an owner, as of real property

Public Pension - monetary benefits to public workers when they retire

Q

Quality - the totality of features and characteristics of a product or service that bear on its ability to satisfy customer's needs or expectations; the degree of excellence produced

Quid-pro-quo - something that is given to you or done for you in return for something you have given or done for someone else

R

Real Useful Value - some things which are needful for life and having practical benefit to human life

Recessions - a period of an economic contraction, sometimes limited in scope or duration

Redistribution - the theory, policy, or practice of lessening or reducing inequalities in income through such measures as progressive income taxation and antipoverty programs

Regulations - a rule or order issued by an executive authority or regulatory agency of a government and having the force of law

Repercussions - an effect or result, often indirect or remote, of some event or action

Resources - a source of supply or support: a natural source of wealth or revenue

Risk - the chance that an investment will lose value

S

Scarcity - insufficiency or shortness of supply; dearth

Socialism - a theory or system of social organization that advocates the ownership and control of the means of production and distribution, capital, land, etc., by the community as a whole, usually through a centralized government

Standard Deviation - a measure of the dispersion of a frequency distribution that is the square root of the arithmetic mean of the squares of the deviation of each of the class frequencies from the arithmetic mean of the frequency distribution

Stock Market - a particular market where stocks and bonds are traded; stock exchange

Subsidy -	a direct monetary aid furnished by a government to private business, a charity organization, or the like
Subsistence Farming -	farming whose products are intended to provide for the basic needs of the farmer, with little surplus for marketing
Supercilious -	coolly and patronizingly haughty
Supply -	a quantity of something on hand or available, as for use; a stock or store

T

Tariff -	a tax required for goods imported or exported
Tax break -	a special tax benefit given to promote specific economic or social objectives
Taxation -	a sum of money demanded by a government for its support or for specific facilities or services, levied upon incomes, property, sales, etc.
Telecommuting -	working from home using internet or phone as means of communication
Tithe -	the tenth part of any thing; but appropriately, the tenth part of the increase and income arising from the profits of land and stock, to be given back to God to show our gratitude toward His abundant blessings
Trade -	the act or process of buying, selling, or exchanging commodities, at either wholesale or retail, within a country or between countries
Trepidation -	a nervous or fearful feeling of uncertain agitation

U

Undercutting Market - to offer goods or services at an unreasonably lower price or rate than (a competing price or rate) or than that of competitor(s)

V

Value - the worth of something in terms of the amount of other things for which it can be exchanged or in terms of some medium of exchange

W

Wealth - all things that have a monetary or exchange value or anything that has utility and is capable of being appropriated or exchanged

Work - to perform or carry through a task requiring sustained effort or continuous repeated operations, a matter of taking dominion of God's world, and providing for human needs

World Gross Product - the combined gross national income of all the countries in the world

ANSWER KEY

INTRODUCTION AND CHAPTER 1

VOCABULARY AND TERMS

1. d
2. c
3. f
4. a
5. b
6. e
7. k
8. h
9. i
10. l
11. g
12. j
13. m

STUDY QUESTIONS

1. Over 2,000 verses in the Bible address the subject of economics.
2. "oikos-despoteo" is translated "keeper of the home" or "one who directs the home's day-to-day activities"
3. The world serves money like they would serve a slave-master.
4. We can recover by returning to biblical principles relating to economics.
5. God is in control. God is the first cause behind all of the movement in the world. Romans 11:36 points out that all things happen "of Him and through Him."
6. Our physical energy comes from the food we eat. These calories give us energy to move around and to think.
7. He is motivated by money and pleasure.
8. They give way to despair and move on to playing games, saturation in entertainment, and pleasure. They seek escape and commit suicide.
9. They hope for more money, and hope that this money will make them happy.
10. To glorify God and to enjoy Him forever.
11. Love for God and love for others.
12. Money or mammon.
13. We are Christ's servants. Answers may vary.
14. We take our paycheck as a gift from God. It is also something we are supposed to steward.
15. Answers:

- #1 - Identify the demand (or market need)
- #2 - Assemble the capital and the know-how, and then apply time and work to produce the product or service.
- #3 - Find the market, and sell the product or service to the market.

LIFE INTEGRATION AND SPIRITUAL APPLICATION

1. Answers may vary.
2. They are expected to work 6 days a week, and rest a seventh day.
3. All was vanity and grasping for the wind.
4. All his days are sorrowful, and his work burdensome; even in the night his heart takes no rest. This also is vanity.
5. He would not be satisfied. The rich man loses sleep. You can't take anything with you. Naked he returns to the dust.
6. The whole duty of man is to fear God and keep His commandments.
7. The rich man wanted access to some of his money, so he could continue to invest it. He wanted the money working for him. He didn't want the money sitting there and not doing anything. The steward returned at least a portion of his money to him. We are stewarding God's money and resources. Answers may vary.
8. The desire to be rich and the love of money.
9. God gives us time and money (and physical energy).
10. Answers may vary.

CHAPTER 2

VOCABULARY AND TERMS

1. j
2. r
3. e
4. c
5. a
6. q
7. i
8. f
9. s
10. d
11. h
12. p
13. b
14. l

15. k
16. o
17. n
18. m
19. g

STUDY QUESTIONS

1. Answers may vary. Food, clothing.
2. Answers may vary. Washing machines, cars, toilets, and electrical devices would be luxuries in 1910.
3. Answers may vary.
4. Answers may vary (depending on time and place of search.) In January, 2022, the average price was $19,800.
5. Answers:

- a. #5 and possibly #9
- b. #1
- c. #7
- d. #2 and possibly #3

6. Discontentment and ingratitude with God's recent provisions. Desiring something that God has not given you the power to get.
7. Worship of materials, wine, food, and money. Greed, lust, discontentment, and ingratitude.
8. The spoiled kid isn't grateful for what he has been given.
9. An auction is a place where multiple people bid on a product, and you get an idea how much people are willing to pay for it.
10. A free market trade occurs when one party gives up something to a second party to get something else the first party wants more than the thing he is giving up.
11. The seller wants to know the highest price the buyer would pay for the stuff he's selling. The buyer wants to pay the lowest price the seller is willing to take for the stuff. And, the buyer might even conceal his own valuation of the product (Proverbs 20:14).
12. The four factors are: 1) Location, 2) Reputation of the seller and quality of his service, 3) Financing Availability, and 4) The Quality of the Product, bells and whistles, the mileage, etc.
13. The supply goes up as the price of a product goes up because suppliers see opportunities to make more money (or profit) on the product.
14. The demand goes down when the price of a product goes up, because there are fewer people who are able or willing to pay that much for the product.
15. The supply goes up as the price of a product goes up because suppliers see opportunities to make more money (or profit) on the product. The demand goes down when the price of a product goes up because there are fewer people who are able or willing to pay that much for the product.
16. Market equilibrium is the point at which the supply of the product (from businesses providing the product) exactly meets the demand for the product at the price people are willing to pay.
17. Elasticity is the degree to which the demand will change if you increase or decrease the price. Hamburgers have high elasticity. Gasoline and oil have low elasticity. Changes in prices of gasoline doesn't increase or decrease the number of people wanting to fill up their cars with gas.
18. Malthus forgot that God is good. He did not believe that the earth had plenty of potential for pro-

ducing more food. He was concerned that the pie of available food would stay the same, and we would all have to take small slices of it. He didn't realize the pie could get bigger and bigger.

19. You need God's resources, labor, tools and capital, creativity and entrepreneurship
20. Answer:

Product	Hours to Make It	Hourly Wage	Labor Costs
House (2000 sq. ft., 186 sq. m.)	2,400 hours	$16.36	$39,264
Autombile, assembly	30 hours	$16.36	$490.80
Kitchen Table	8 hours	$16.36	$130.88
Deck (300 sq ft. 28 sq. m.	120 hours	$16.36	$1963.20

21. God brings forth the increase.

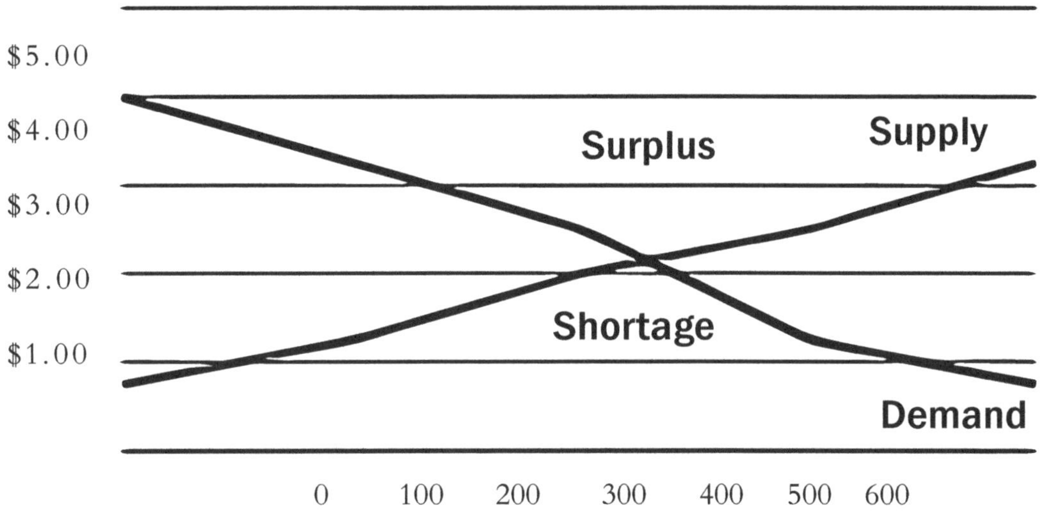

SUPPLY AND DEMAND EXERCISE

1. Answer:

- Shortage shading under curves
- Surplus shading over curves
- a. At a price of $1.00, there would be a shortage.
- b. 325 cups of lemonade under.
- c. At a price of $4.00 there would be a surplus.
- d. 250 cups of lemonade over.
- e. Equilibrium is approximately 315 cups of lemonade.

2. Answer:

Product	Demand Change	Price Change	Elasticity	Elastic or Inelastic?
Luxury Diamonds	-5%	30%	0.17	Inelastic
Gas	10%	-30%	0.33	Inelastic
Salt	-10%	20%	0.5	Inelastic
Instant Coffee	50%	30%	1.67	Elastic
Baked Beans	100%	-25%	4	Elastic
Financial Magazine	-30%	10%	3	Elastic

LIFE INTEGRATION AND SPIRITUAL APPLICATION

1. Answers may vary.
2. Answers may vary.
3. Answers may vary.
4. Answers may vary.
5. Answers may vary.
6. Answers may vary.

CHAPTER 3

VOCABULARY

1. k
2. d
3. h
4. l
5. c
6. i
7. e
8. a
9. g
10. b
11. j
12. f

STUDY QUESTIONS

1. God provides the power and ability for any nation to make wealth. If 300 million people have the

motivation to work hard mentally and physically, God has enabled that.

2. That nation will be cursed materially.
3. Work six days, and rest a seventh.
4. Lots of people working hard (both mentally and physically).
5. You will save $3,960 in the construction of one home. The nation saves $1,980,000,000 each year using nail guns. You would save $3,710 if you purchase a nail gun for building a single home.
6. This refers to working efficiently and discovering creative new ways to do the work.
7. Corrupt governments slow everything down by red tape, bribery, and regulations.
8. There was not enough division of labor. When everybody was just getting by in the farming work, there wasn't much time to do anything else.
9. The development of the plow, the weaving machine, the reaper, and the nail gun.
10. The price of the nail dropped from 2 cents to 0.2 cents per nail (a 90% savings). The first mass production of nails occurred in the 1750s.
11. God owns the world. Unbelievers disagree. They may think nobody owns the world or has a right to it. They may think that man owns it, or governments own the land.
12. We are stewards appointed to take care of God's land, animals, trees, and crops. Each of us is assigned to take care of the resources, money, and land given us.
13. The 8th commandment, "Thou shalt not steal," establishes the right to own private property.
14. When you don't take care of your house, it may be destroyed by termites and carpenter ants. It may be destroyed by water damage. When you don't change the oil in your car, the engine will eventually be ruined. Most cars will be ruined after about 35,000 miles, if the oil is never changed.
15. God's Word, godliness, contentment, loving God, and worshiping Him.
16. Sweden, the UK, Australia, Canada, and the US.
17. The apple merchant cheats by putting a hand on the scale and making it look like the buyer is getting 25 pounds of apples when he is really only getting 20 pounds. The buyer cheats by shaving a little silver off the coin he uses to pay for the apples.
18. The love of money.
19. Some businessmen will continually borrow money to build their "empires." Some will gamble on the stock market, buying and selling quickly in hopes that the markets will rise and fall in their favor. Others will gamble their money in card games and casinos.
20. We give way to burnout and long term inefficiencies. We also cheat God of a day of worship and thanksgiving, and a testimony of faith (or trust in God).
21. These nations are impoverished and under the judgment of God.
22. Answers:

- a. Japan.
- b. The US
- c. Afghanistan
- d. Russia is doing the best. Japan and the US are doing the worst.

LIFE INTEGRATION AND SPIRITUAL APPLICATION

1. Answers will vary.
2. Answers will vary.
3. Answers will vary.
4. We work for the Lord Jesus Christ. We do this not as man-pleasers, but in sincerity of heart, fearing God.
5. That wealth will quickly diminish.
6. Consider whether you are able to steward the money or resources.
7. The slothful man gets discouraged quickly when he runs into a tough problem. The slothful man is not conscientious and meticulous in his work. Answers will vary.
8. Ten percent. Giving less is robbing God.

CHAPTER 4

VOCABULARY AND TERMS

1. l
2. e
3. m
4. c
5. j
6. k
7. d
8. a
9. h
10. f
11. b
12. g
13. i

STUDY QUESTIONS

1. The fall brought thorns and thistles - an increase in the amount of work required to yield fruit and get the job done.
2. The house would be filled with spiderwebs, dust and dirt, dead insects, and animal droppings. Water damage would doubtless rot out the floors, and the paint would fade on the siding and internal walls.
3. Evil civil governments and foolish policies on the part of these governments brought about the famines of the 20th century.
4. In large part, the African famines were due to droughts and poor economies. Also, corrupt governments and a thieving populace make it hard for an entrepreneurial farmer to get ahead. Class envy, socialist policies, red tape, and bribery keep farming from developing.
5. 355 million metric tons per year. 600 million metric tons in
6. . That would last about 1.75 years.

7. 0.3%
8. God sends His sunshine and rain on the just and unjust. He also protects nations from terrible tyrants who would destroy them.
9. Divorce, disease, debt, and slavery.
10. Seven years.
11. The Muslims were enslaving Europeans as far north as Norway and Sweden.
12. Pope Nicholas V. Charles II and James II.
13. William Wilberforce
14. By the regenerating work of the Holy Spirit in the hearts of men
15. The man is impoverished, and he cannot afford to buy shoes for his children or put a roof over their heads.
16. They want to go into debt to make a lot of money quickly. They can do this when inflation is causing the value of money to diminish.
17. He has to borrow $180,000.
- Inflation: He adds $50,000 to his $20,000. He made $50,000 from inflation.
- Deflation: He lost $50,000. He has to pay the bank $30,000 out of his own pocket.
18. A wicked ruler is like a roaring lion and a charging bear. He does a lot of damage to economies, and it is usually the poor that suffer the most because of it.
19. Ten righteous men. 4,000 faithful Christians might save Los Angeles from destruction (using a similar ratio).
20. The United States, the Netherlands, Switzerland, and England. The Protestant Christian faith has dominated in these countries.
21. These countries begin to break God's commandments, more and more. They begin to cheat, lie, and steal. Labor-management relationships break down.

LIFE INTEGRATION AND SPIRITUAL APPLICATION

1. We deduce that slavery is a curse because this first mention of slavery in the Bible is attached to a curse.
2. The transgressions of the people result in more princes and government. You can help reduce tyranny by self-government or ceasing from transgressions.
3. His descendants will be mighty in the earth. Wealth and riches will be in his house. He will be in everlasting remembrance. He will not be afraid of bad news. His characteristics: He fears the Lord. He delights greatly in the commandments of God. His heart is steadfast, trusting the Lord. He is gracious. He lends to the poor. He distributes freely to the poor.
4. Jesus has come to bring righteousness and peace. He delivers the needy and the poor. He has brought more abundance of food. And He overcomes His enemies.
5. Use it up. Wear it out. Make it do, or do without.

CHAPTER 5

VOCABULARY

1. c
2. m
3. o
4. l
5. h
6. e
7. n
8. b
9. k
10. f
11. i
12. a
13. j
14. d
15. g

STUDY QUESTIONS

1. Conquest, plunder, and enslavement.
2. Biblical law, liberty, property, and industriousness.
3. Feudalism
4. Serfs were renters and sometimes they owned their own property. They gave of their proceeds and volunteered for the king's army, in exchange for military protection of their families and lands. The feudal system was far better than the slave-based systems of the pagan world.
5. Lords and noblemen served the king. But they also had some representative powers, mostly provided by the Magna Carta of 1215.
6. Self-interest. People receive rewards for the work they do. The fundamental motive for Christians in their work and service must be love for God, love for others, and a sense of duty to make use of time and talents (as a good steward).
7. Private people and private companies or partnerships of free people own the businesses (in a capitalist economy).
8. The fundamental shift in the Industrial Revolution was that the factory replaced the family as the primary means of production.
9. The percentage of families living on farms in the US dropped from 26.7% to 1.6% (between 1920 and 2020).
10. Capitalism is primarily interested in maximizing efficiency (and making money) as the highest value. The Bible places loving God and loving our neighbor as the higher value. Organizing society around

economic incentive has contributed to the breakdown of moral and ethical limits that used to govern the Christian West.

11. Answers:

- a. Socialism
- b. Communism
- c. Communism
- d. Capitalism
- e. Capitalism
- f. Communism
- g. Socialism

12. Answers:

- a. $56,310.
- b. $240
- c. Americans are doing 234 times better than Cubans.

13. Worker ownership of the means of production.

14. Answers:

- Communism: The government owns factories and farms.
- Capitalism: Rich capitalists own factories and farms.
- Distributism: Families/workers own factories and farms.

15. The husband and the wife are the economic unit.

16. Education, discipleship, apprenticeship, work, hospitality, charity, recreation, and care for one another.

17. Distributism is the most helpful, and communism or socialism is the most hurtful.

18. Karl Marx said, "Blessed is he who has no family."

19. Karl Marx said his objective in life was to "dethrone God and destroy capitalism."

20. Capitalism provides opportunities for some individuals or even families to make a lot of money. But capitalism can undermine the bonds of family life.

21. Often children and the elderly are turned over to others to take care of. The state usually steps in to take care of the children (through day care and public school programs) and the elderly (through social security). So capitalist systems turn into socialist systems (eventually).

22. Answers:

- a. Socialism emphasizes equality
- b. Capitalism emphasizes efficiency
- c. Biblical Economics emphasizes love and relationships

23. Answers may vary. Self-government and healthy families are essential for liberty. Ownership of property means people are taking responsibility. Freedom from corporate management usually contributes to valuing liberty from tyrannical civil governments.

24. Families are loyal to one another. Family economies are stable. They are more insulated from shocks to the global economy and changing winds of political sentiment.

LIFE INTEGRATION AND SPIRITUAL APPLICATION

1. Answers will vary.
2. The early church combined their resources voluntarily. Socialism is the forced redistribution of wealth. The early church sold property during a time of great distress. This was shortly before AD 70 when Jerusalem was invaded by Rome and completely destroyed.
3. Answers will vary.

CHAPTER 6

VOCABULARY

1. o
2. g
3. q
4. a
5. n
6. c
7. m
8. f
9. h
10. b
11. j
12. i
13. l
14. d
15. k
16. e
17. p

STUDY QUESTIONS

1. 43% of the world is self-employed. 6% of Americans are self-employed.
2. God wants us to work six days and rest a seventh.
3. Economists define work as the necessary labor to keep people alive in a community. From a biblical perspective, work is the necessary cultivation and care of God's material creation for the benefit of one's family and community. Biblical Christians see work as a cultivation and care of God's material creation. Secular economists do not acknowledge God as Creator.
4. Good work or effective work is producing decent quality and quantity in the business accomplished.
5. Church ministry work is primarily concerned with feeding the souls of men, not their bodies. Ministry might also include charitable work—caring for the poor, working in orphanages, etc. Often,

people are not paid for doing ministry work. They do it voluntarily. Business work is compensated by money.

6. The character of each successive generation got worse and worse. Young people didn't get married. They didn't want to have children anymore.
7. These forms of work break down into bond slavery, hired servanthood, apprenticeships, and business ownership. There is also part-time labor, temporary labor, and full-time labor. There is entrepreneurial work, trade business work, franchise work, government work, and corporate work.
8. Answers:
- a. Trade Business
- b. Entrepreneurship
- c. Franchise
- d. Corporate Stock Ownership
- e. Entrepreneurship
- f. Trade Business
9. Common stockholders have a vote on company matters, while preferred stockholders do not. Also, preferred stockholders usually receive a pre-determined dividend at a set interest rate. Common stockholders get a variable amount depending on how well the company did in a given year.
10. While the Word of God discourages debt (especially for the rich). God's law does not allow governments to favor the poor (Ex. 23:3; 30:15). At the same time, God's law forbids government subsidies or special favors for wealthy men and big corporations (Lev. 19:15; Jas. 2:1-4). Such favorable treatment is stealing. It is what the Scriptures refer to as "the respect of persons."
11. By getting into a lot of debt and selling stock, you can access quick capital, undercut the market on prices, mass produce your product, and beat the little guys who are trying to compete.
12. Rockefeller had come up with creative and efficient ways to process oil. It was his innovation that enabled him to lower the price of oil and capture a large percentage of the market.
13. Chapter 11 Bankruptcy
14. Entrepreneurs start up their own businesses, requiring a lot of creativity and risk. They usually work on developing a new product or service. The self-employed person is usually relying on a product or service already developed. They might purchase a franchise. Or they might get involved in network marketing. Or they might work in the trades, where a product or service has already been developed.
15. Answers:
- a. Family-owned businesses and small businesses provide the backbone of a free market economy. They tend to be more stable in difficult economic times.
- b. More self-employment in an economy decentralizes power and wealth.
- c. Self-employment can increase freedom for those who get out from under corporate structures. The self-employed can make their own decisions for their own lives.
- d. Self-employment allows for the development of a family economy, where whole families can work together as a team.
16. Answers:
- a. Self-employment usually doesn't give you a steady paycheck.

- b. Self-employed people can work themselves too hard out of sheer greed. The Bible requires one rest day in seven. But since the amount of money self-employed people make usually depends on how hard they work, they will sometimes work too many hours.
- c. A self-employed person usually has to be a jack-of-all-trades.
- d. Most countries or states require a lot of paperwork from self-employed people. In some cases, small businesses have to withhold income taxes for their employees (including the owners) every month. This usually requires filing a form each month.

17. Your goal is to do everything with all your heart as unto the Lord Jesus Christ. Remember, in everything you do every day, you are a servant of Christ. You represent Him in your attitude, your work, your relationships, and the jobs you do.

LIFE INTEGRATION AND SCRIPTURAL APPLICATION

1. Smartphone and internet surfing is the most notorious time bandit. The average person wastes 145 minutes a day on social media like Facebook and Snapchat. The second most common form of time wasting is gossip. The third big time waster is meetings. And the fourth is daydreaming and lack of focus. Answers will vary
2. The man who kindled the fire is responsible. By God's law, those responsible for making decisions not to correct problems or make proper inspections should be held liable.
3. The wicked do not repay when they file bankruptcy, or when they incorporate and walk away from their debts (while leaving the company liable for the debts).
4. Answers will vary.
5. Answers will vary.
6. Answers will vary.
7. Answers will vary.

CHAPTER 7

VOCABULARY

1. e
2. k
3. d
4. j
5. l
6. c
7. i
8. f
9. m
10. h
11. a

12. o
13. b
14. g
15. n
16. p

STUDY QUESTIONS

1. Money is a store of material value and a means to facilitate trade.
2. Answers may vary slightly

Type of Money	Price Stability	Scarcity	Universal Desirability	Divisibility	Portability	Durability
Paper	Yes	No	Yes	Yes	No	No
Fish	No	No	No	Yes	No	No
Gold	Yes	Yes	Yes	Yes	Yes	Yes
Silver	Yes	Yes	Yes	Yes	Yes	Yes
Pianos	Yes	Yes	No	No	No	Yes
Salt	No	No	Yes	Yes	No	No
Crypto-currency	No	Yes	No	Yes	Yes	Yes

3. Money is a convenient medium of exchange for buying stuff. Money is a good way to measure value. Money provides a place to store wealth with the hope that it won't lose value over time.
4. Burying tools in the ground is a waste of those tools. They should be used to build something productive. Money is a tool and should not be buried in the ground.
5. Answers:
- Rent in 2020 — 1/3 ounce of gold
- Rent in 1880 — 1/3 ounce of gold
- Rent in 1768 — a little less than 1/2 ounce of gold
6. Abraham paid 400 shekels (or 100 ounces) of silver or $2,500 for the cave of Machpelah.
7. 8,000 different types of currency or coin.
8. Answers:
- 1st - the scale is biased in favor of one party
- 2nd - Shaving off a little piece of the silver or gold in the coin
- 3rd - Changing the quality of the substance being traded without the purchaser realizing it

9. They would mix lower quality substances like tin, lead, or copper into the silver or gold.
10. The first cheaters who spend the first cheap coins (while prices are low) get the most stuff. The first person to be robbed is the seller who receives the cheapened coins for his products. Those who are hurt the most are those who collect the debased coins and keep them in savings. These are usually widows who live off their savings.
11. Bouncing a check happens when you write a check for a certain amount of money when you don't have that amount of money in your checking account.
12. Paper money were notes issued by banks (or other institutions), exchangeable for the amount of gold or silver contained on the note itself.
13. King Louis XIV tried counterfeiting for the first time around AD 1700. Abraham Lincoln attempted it in the 1860s.
14. 1974
15. They charge interest from those who borrow money from the bank.
16. $15,000. $1,250 per month.
17. $3,000. The bank is profiting $12,000 per year when it lends out your money.
18. It was immune from state-based taxation and its major client was the US federal government.
19. The national bank got a little too greedy and proceeded to lend out more money than it held in deposits (in gold and silver coins).
20. 1950.
21. 1968. It appeared deceitful because the silver certificates and the non-backed certificates (dollar bills) looked almost exactly alike.
22. Answers:

- 1. The US Federal Reserve could issue money by buying federal government debt (bonds).
- 2. The Federal Reserve Board has also been given the power to control every bank in the country by setting the Reserve Requirement Ratio.
- 3. The US Federal Reserve also has huge control over the interest rates at which Americans borrow money. Commercial banks borrow money from the federal reserve when money is tight. And the federal reserve board is in charge of setting this reserve rate.

23. Answers:

- Household debt — 43% - 80%. (almost doubled)
- Business debt - 31% - 50%. (increased by 67%)
- Federal debt - 32% - 133% (increased four fold)

24. Answers:

- 1980 — 2%
- 2008 - 8%
- 2021 - 18%

25. Companies would artificially prop up the value of the stock by buying their own stock. As they invested in their own stock using easy debt money, the stock would rise. This would incite other investors to jump back into the market to purchase the company's stock.
26. Apple Computer contributed $85.5 billion in stock buybacks. Apple Computer's stock increased

from $38 to $182 between 2019 and 2021 (a 4-fold increase).

27. Answer:

	1930	2020	Ratio
Gallon of Milk	$0.30	$2.50	8.3
Gallon of Gas	$0.20	$3.50	17.5
Average Income	$1400	$62,000	44.3

28. Part of the increase is due to inflation, and the other part is due to an improved standard of living. Improved technology and automated manufacturing have improved the standard of living quite a lot since the early 1900s. The main reason for inflation is that governments spend themselves into a lot of debt.

29. Answers:

- a. $1,000
- b. $2,000
- c. $1,000
- d. They thought the king had given them free money, fully $1.00.
- e. 33 cents in value was stolen from each person (each of which had $1.00 at the beginning).

30. $8.5 trillion.

31. Answers:

- a. $1,000,000.
- b. $2,000,000
- c. $1,000,000
- d. The king's assets increased in value from $1,000,000 to $3,000,000. They increased because the money supply in the community increased from $1,000,000 to $3,000,000.
- e. They lost 67% in value. They were given 2% interest in the first. year. So they lost 65% on their investment in the first year.

32. 82% of American families with children were on welfare. Altogether, at least 75% of Americans were on welfare by 2021.

33. It would be harder to counterfeit gold because it has a certain look, a certain hardness, and a certain weight to it that would be hard to replace with some other substance.

LIFE INTEGRATION AND SPIRITUAL APPLICATION

1. 1. Answers may vary.
2. Answers:

- a. David wants to be delivered from people who speak lying words and people whose right hand is a right hand of dishonesty or falsehood.

- b. An honest society looks like: Sons are as fruitful plants grown up in their youth; Daughters are as pillars, sculptured in palace style; Our barns are full, supplying all kinds of produce; Our sheep reproduce, bringing forth thousands and ten thousands in our fields; Our oxen may be well laden, and there will be no breaking in (stealing) or going out (lost oxen/sheep)
- c. Answers may vary.

3. Answers:

- a. The love of money.
- b. There has been too much love for money, which is the root of all evil (1 Tim. 6:10). Covetousness lurks in the heart. Self-centeredness prevails. And people want to get rich quickly.

CHAPTER 8

VOCABULARY

1. m
2. e
3. l
4. a
5. k
6. i
7. f
8. r
9. b
10. j
11. g
12. n
13. c
14. p
15. h
16. d
17. t
18. s
19. q
20. o

STUDY QUESTIONS

1. 180 cows from 3 mama cows in twenty years.
2. Answers:

- a. $100
- b. $200

- c. $2400
- d. $300
- e. $2000
- f. $0
- g. $0
- h. $4400

3. Answers:

- a. The saver made $80.61, but appeared to make $220.71.
- b. The saver lost $33.24, but appeared to make $22.02.

4. Answers:

- a. 82 hours.
- b. $232,946.87. This does not include the last $12,057.60 of interest. If you include the last $12,057.60 in interest, the total would be $245,004.47.
- c. Answers may vary. He could go to college and work another job.
- d. Answers may vary. But, most young men and women have a hard time saving money, and they waste a lot of time.

5. Government bonds are a safe investment because governments usually don't go bankrupt. They can raise taxes to pay their bonds (if they want to).
6. Government bond rates often do not keep up with inflation, so they make for a bad investment.
7. You would charge a higher interest because you are taking a chance that the irresponsible lender would (at some point) be incapable of paying back on the loan.
8. Answers:

- a-2
- b-3
- c-1

9. Investors earn dividends. And investors can sell their stock for a profit (for a higher price than what they paid for it).
10. A legitimate reason to invest in the stock market is to take dominion of God's world, make good use of money, and invest in a company's gainful work and production of helpful resources for consumers.
11. A bad reason (often motivating day traders) is to invest in stocks to get rich quick.
12. If you are going to own part of a company, you want to be sure that it's a good company and that it isn't overvalued compared to other companies like it. You would want to know how much profit the company made over the last five years before you invested in it.
13. He purchases the stock for $35, and immediately sells it for $45. He has earned $2,000. Subtracting the $200, the options trader has walked away with $1,800. During the first nine months of 2021, $6.9 trillion of options exchanged hands, while only $5.8 trillion in stocks were traded. That means more business was conducted in the arena of gambling than in the arena of real investment. Tesla was the most popular stock in the gambling/options market.
14. When the Price to Earnings ratio rises above 15, the investors are more interested in price (and a quick profit in turn over of the stock) than they are in the earnings (or the productivity of the company).
15. Five years.

16. Your best investment is your own business. Your very best investment is to lay up treasures in heaven, to give up something for the cause of Christ. Visiting the poor, helping the "least of these" - the needy brothers and sisters of Christ in the church- is your very best investment.
17. The problem with the rich man in Jesus' parable was that he had the opportunity to help Lazarus every day for a long time, but he didn't help the single case that presented itself to him.
18. You can use land for agriculture and grazing. You can build houses, offices, or warehouses on the land and rent out the buildings. You can sometimes improve on the property for a profit.
19. Some renters not paying the rent. The rentals requiring upkeep (or maintenance). Also, most people have to go into debt to purchase property. If property values go down, you may lose your investment (and all the capital you put into it).
20. Charlotte NC, Orlando, FL, and Atlanta, GA are the three best places. San Francisco, CA, Los Angeles, CA, and Seattle WA are the worst places.
21. Gold and silver are better seen as money, or a place in which to hold value. Putting your savings into gold and silver won't give you a return on your investment. This won't produce an increase, or provide a service, or manufacture products that would be a help to others.
22. In the case of inflation: You would make $20,000 on your $10,000 investment. That's 200% in three years, or a 67% return (per year). In the case of deflation: You would lose $20,000. You would owe the bank $10,000.
23. Do not live beyond your means. Save money to make your purchases. If at all possible, purchase your first home (as a very small home) valued at 1.25 times your annual salary.
24. Most of the countries of Africa as well as the Bahamas, Belize, and El Salvador.
25. It would take 20 months to save up for the car—or 1 year and 8 months.
26. The tortoise favored focus, consistency, and perseverance over speed.
27. $76.50 is taken out for Social Security and Medicare. Technically, $38.25 is taken out of your paycheck, and $38.25 is provided by your company.
28. Honesty. Good accounting presents an honest look at a company's finances.
29. The IRA and 401(k) are tax-deferred savings. Most income is taxed, which means that you have to pay federal and state income tax on that money. With the IRA and 401(k) you can defer paying taxes on the money until you are 65 or older. The assumption is that you will be earning less money during your later years, your retirement years, and therefore have to pay less taxes on the money drawn from your IRA or 401(k) accounts.
30. You would have to save $480,000.

LIFE INTEGRATION AND SPIRITUAL APPLICATION

1. Answers may vary.
2. Answers may vary.
3. Fear of losing money and greed. Answers may vary. Fear of God, gratitude to God, contentment for God's gifts, and a realization of God's sovereignty (that all is in God's hands).

4. 10% of your income to the church. 3.33% of your income to the poor in your neighborhood. And the edges of the field, a small portion of your produce should be made available for the poor in the area. Answers may vary.
5. The general principle for giving is not to pass up any opportunity for helping somebody out that immediately presents itself to you. Your neighbor is the person who you happen to run into on a journey, at work, at the market, or in your neighborhood. Answers may very.
6. A good man saves an inheritance for his grandchildren. And, children should take care of their aging parents and grandparents. The world's system encourages the elderly to use up their inheritance, and for children and grandchildren to turn their aging parents and grandparents over to the government for their care and upkeep.

CHAPTER 9

VOCABULARY AND TERMS

1. n
2. k
3. f
4. a
5. d
6. l
7. e
8. b
9. g
10. i
11. c
12. h
13. m
14. j

STUDY QUESTIONS

1. Governments can stay out of the way to help the free market economy (and keep taxes low).
2. God's established purpose for governments is to use the sword on the person who commits criminal deeds
3. 85%.

4. Answers:

North Korea	Communist
Turkmenistan	Muslim (89%)
South Sudan	Roman Catholic (37%), Anglican (18%)
Venezuela	Roman Catholic (96%)
Eritrea	Eritrean Orthodox (35%), Muslim (37%)

5. Answers:

Denmark	Protestant (75%)
Norway	Protestant (69%)
Finland	Protestant (69%)
New Zealand	Protestant (46%)
Sweden	Protestant (60%)

6. Between 1996 and 2000.
7. Lockheed Martin
8. $52 billion in the COVID-19 shots. $14 million in campaign donations. That's a ratio of 371.
9. By a factor of about 8-9.
10. Some big cities like San Francisco and New York City limit the amount of rent landlords can charge for their apartments.
11. The decision to lockdown the world during Covid-19 resulted in a 3.1% drop in the gross world product, the largest drop in world productivity since the 1800s.
12. Los Angeles in 1908.
13. $287.5 Billion
14. Biggest increases in the US federal government revenues occurred during Abraham Lincoln's era (1860), Woodrow Wilson's era (1912-1920), and Franklin D. Roosevelt's era (1930-1946).
15. Answers:

- 10% x $20,000 = $2,000
- 12% x $60,000 = $7,200
- 22% x $20,000 = $4,400
- Total tax = $13,600

16. Wyoming or Alaska may be the most favorable for people who desire lower taxes.

State	Sales Tax (Mark None)	Property Tax (Mark Lowest)	Income Tax (Mark None
Wyoming		Lowest	None
Washington			None
Texas			None
Alaska	None		None
Oregon	None		
New Hampshire	None		
Montana	None		

State	Sales Tax (Mark None)	Property Tax (Mark Lowest)	Income Tax (Mark None
Louisiana		Lowest	
Alabama		Lowest	

17. Answers:

- a. The US governments (federal/state/local) are 50 times larger than the Roman government during the time of Christ.
- b. About 25 times larger than when the nation was founded in 1780.

18. Answers:

- a. Maintain the overall ratio of the people's income dedicated to taxation (at all levels of government) at well under 10%.
- b. Incorporate a flat tax in amount (not percentage). If a poor man earning $15,000 per year pays $1,000 per year in taxes, a rich man earning $1,000,000 per year should pay the same amount of money.
- c. Prefer forms of taxation that are not attached to income or property. These are the worst forms of taxation. Sales tax and poll taxes (in which one has to pay a tax to vote) would be preferred.
- d. Eliminate all inheritance taxation and property taxation.

19. Answers:

- a. For the five most free nations in the world, the average GDP per person is $72,715.40.
- b. For the five least free nations in the world, the average GDP per person is $2,300.20.
- c. The economy of the five most free nations is 32 times better than the enslaved nations (controlled by tyrannical governments).
- d. Asia - Singapore
- Oceania - New Zealand
- Western Europe - Switzerland
- Northern Europe - Ireland
- Eastern Europe - Estonia
- North America - Canada (or US)
- South America - Chile

20. Beginning in the year 2006, freedoms started to disappear from the world.

21. The purpose of the World Bank is to loan money to poor countries over which a world government might extend its control. The real purpose for handing out money to poor countries is in order to control these countries.

22. Answers:

- a. When a business is aiding an enemy government with military trade secrets or armaments. This especially applies to wartime.
- b. When a business deceives its customers in advertising and contracts, and it does not fulfill its commitments.

- c. When a business tries to ruin another business by violence or robbery.
- d. When a business knowingly avoids safety measures, and employees
- get hurt and or killed.
- e. When a business provides unfair access to critical information about the business to some investors but not to others. All investors should have equal access to information about the business that appears positive (and would increase the stock price) or negative (that would decrease the stock price). The U. S. Securities and Exchange Commission (SEC) will investigate companies that are not providing fair access to information for their investors.

23. Comunist China as well as the Muslim countries of Morocco, Kazakhstan, United Arab Emirates, Indonesia, and Malaysia. The Roman Catholic countries of Mexico and Peru also ranked among the most dishonest. Switzerland, Norway, Denmark, Netherlands, and Sweden were the most honest countries, registering the highest percentage of wallets returned.

LIFE INTEGRATION AND SPIRITUAL APPLICATION

1. Answers:
- a. Civil penalty for gross negligence resulting in death is capital punishment.
- b. No.
- c. 350.
- d. $20 billion.
- e. Answers may vary.
2. Answers:
- a. High property taxes requiring the enslavement of children to the state (or sending children off to government controlled facilities for instruction and service). Also, taxation that exceeds 10%.
- b. Our governments have exceeded the biblical limit by 8-10%. To include debt, that ratio would be more like 23%.
- c. We can cry out to God. Answers may vary.
3. Answers will vary.
4. Answers will vary. Christians should think twice before they make a gigantic fire in their yard that might cause ash to fall on their neighbor's home and property. They should be very careful never to litter or to allow debris to blow off their pickup truck as they drive down the road. They would be careful to place coverings over deep holes in their yard so people won't fall into them. They would put fences around a swimming pool so a two-year-old neighbor doesn't fall into it and drown. They would build their homes using safety standards such that the second floor doesn't collapse when twenty people are congregating there.

CHAPTER 10

VOCABULARY

1. i
2. k
3. f

4. a
5. b
6. c
7. j
8. l
9. g
10. d
11. h
12. e
13. n
14. m

STUDY QUESTIONS

1. Answers will vary.
2. The fear of God as the beginning of wisdom is missing.
3. Biblically, the fundamental issue is to tell the truth. As we commend others for the work they do, we must still recognize that all gifts come from God. Thus, a man-centered view in gaining success in business still won't recognize God as the source of blessing or give Him the thanksgiving and praise for it.
4. The confidence of the unbeliever is in himself. The confidence of the believer is in God.
5. Gal. 6:7, Prov. 12:11, 14
6. Answers:
- a. Don't procrastinate - Ecclesiastes 9:10
- b. Use your resources. Don't be a miser. - Proverbs 11:24-25
- c. Be diligent. - Proverbs 13:4
- d. Work in spite of obstacles. - Proverbs 20:4
- e. Prioritize the important things in life. - Luke 10:38-42
- f. Listen to correction. - Proverbs 13:18
7. 7. Obeying God's commandments.
8. Joseph's father trusted him with the sheep business. Potiphar trusted him with his agricultural businesses. The prison director trusted him with the prisoners. And the Pharaoh trusted him with running the entire national economy.
9. Joseph demonstrated an overall optimistic and hopeful attitude. And, Joseph was an honest employee, not because his manager was watching him but because God was watching him.
10. When Joseph insisted on moral integrity in relation to Potiphar's wife, he paid for it by serving four to ten years in an Egyptian prison.
11. About 78% of business owners surveyed by the Fundbox polling organization said they can't write their own paychecks because of this problem. Another 23% can't buy needed equipment or hire new employees because their customers are so slow at paying invoices.
12. They might say something like, "My competitor's products are junk. They always do sloppy work.

Their customer service is worthless." Or they might mention a weak element of a competitor's product or character and then forget to point out the strengths or benefits that outweigh the drawbacks.

13. Answers:

- a. Strive to understand the real need of the customer, and fill that need. Be sure that the sale and your profit is not your number one goal in the conversation. A good salesman isn't going to be talking the whole time. He's asking questions. He's attempting to provide needed expertise that would assist the customer. The goal of the company is to satisfy the customer, but also to surprise the customer with a better product or service than the customer expected to receive.
- b. Be truthful in the presentation of the product or service. To the extent that the product will not fulfill the customer's needs, he should know it. While it is okay to highlight the better features of your product, don't use the better features to cover up the worse.
- c. Focus on quality. Instead of worrying about your competitors or hard selling your customers, just work on giving your customers the best product possible.

14. The Chick-fil-A company maintained unmatched quality of service for decades. The customer experience was always top notch.

15. "Sell good merchandise at a reasonable profit, treat your customers like human beings, and they will always come back for more." The company insisted on 100% customer satisfaction.

16. At the least, quality products will conform to stated requirements or specifications. Negatively stated, quality seeks to produce products and services free from defects or any characteristic that may be disappointing to the customer.

17. Their goal is to produce almost exactly the same standard of product every time. They do not want variation between the products or the food served. The customer expects a certain taste, a certain look, or a certain function with each product or meal purchased. They want the same hamburger in size, taste, and appearance, whether they purchase it in Denver, Colorado or Miami, Florida. They want the business to provide the same specifications in all the important features of the product, with minimal variation.

18. Answers:

- Chart 1: Accuracy is high. Precision is Low.
- Chart 2: Accuracy is Low. Precision is high.

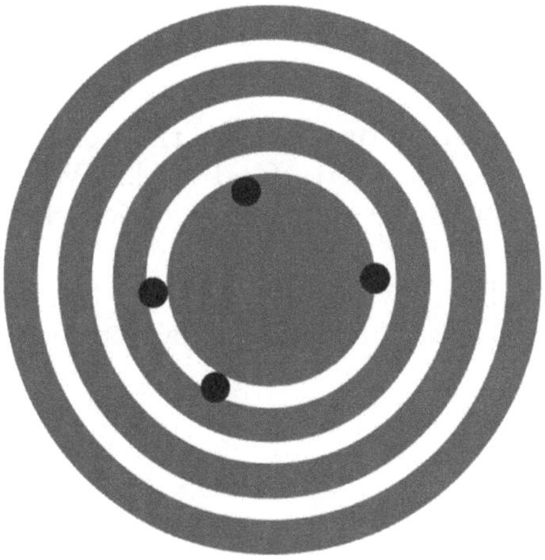

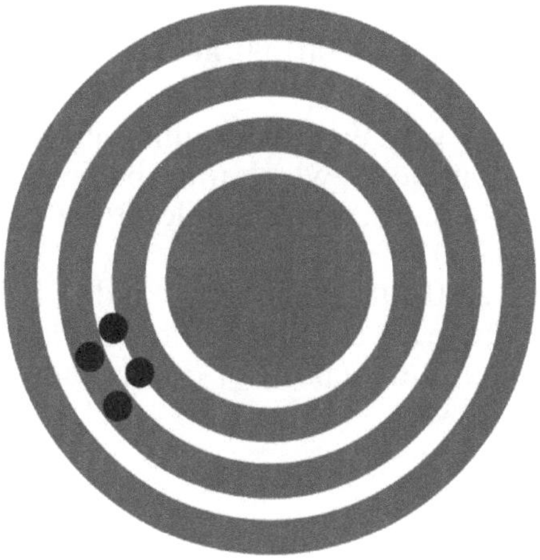

	Machine 1	Machine 2	Machine 3
	9.44	9.52	9.45
	9.44	9.51	9.45
	9.45	9.48	9.46
	9.46	9.43	9.46
	9.46	9.42	9.48
	9.51	9.47	9.50
	9.52	9.48	9.50
	9.44	9.49	9.47
	9.48	9.51	9.47
	9.52	9.47	9.50
Average (Mean)	9.472	9.478	9.474
Target	9.478	9.47 inches	9.47 inches
How many bad balls?	2	2	0
Average deviation	0.0284	0.0244	0.0168

19. Answers:

- c. Machine 1 came closest to the target of 9.47.
- d. Machine 3 had the smallest deviation
- e. Machine 3 was the best machine, with zero bad balls.

LIFE INTEGRATION AND SPIRITUAL APPLICATION

1. Answers may vary. Wisdom begins with fear of God or reverence for God. The right character, disposition, and outlook—which must be formed in humility and the fear of God—is key. Wisdom makes the right decisions, treats people in the right way, and retains the right perspective, whether things are going right or not.
2. Reading 1,000 success books wouldn't help that much. The key to success is the fear of God and humility. These are character traits. Reading success books doesn't necessarily develop the fear of God and humility in the character of someone.
3. Answers will vary.
4. Answers will vary.
5. Answers will vary.
6. Answers will vary.
7. Answers will vary.

CHAPTER 11

STUDY QUESTIONS

1. Either they can earn more money or just spend less.
2. Housing, transportation, and insurance (medical is most of it).
3. You should be willing to pay $400 for a higher quality bicycle that would last 4-times longer.
4. The Toyota Land Cruiser and the Toyota Sequoia.
5. The Honda Odyssey and Toyota Avalon.
6. The Ford Escape loses about $6,000 in value in the first year. From the graph it appears the 1st year and the 5th year are the best purchase points.
7. The Jeep Wrangler is the best. The Nissan Leaf is the worst.
8. The Toyota Camry. Maintenance costs were much lower.
9. You can run a vehicle history report on the car.
10. Automobiles and insurance are your biggest expenses when you are just starting out in life.
11. Using a Christian Medical Sharing ministry, that single person would pay only about $2,000 per year, and the family would pay $6,000 per year.
12. $760 per year.
13. Unplug the appliance.
14. Heating and air conditioning is the biggest energy cost.
15. Some homes have been used to manufacture drugs, and it might be impossible to remove the toxic conditions residing in the walls and the floors. Mold is a major problem in some areas of the country. Radon levels may be too high.
16. Answers:

- a. $104 per month, $1,248 per year
- b. $60 per month, $300 per year
- c. $760 per year
- d. $4,000 per year
- e. $610 per year

- f. $416 per year

17. $7,334 per year, which would amount to $88,008 in ten years.

LIFE INTEGRATION AND SPIRITUAL APPLICATION

1. Answers will vary.
2. Answers will vary.
3. Answers will vary.
4. Answers will vary.

CHAPTER 12

VOCABULARY

1. e
2. k
3. d
4. i
5. f
6. a
7. h
8. j
9. b
10. g
11. c

STUDY QUESTIONS

1. A receipt.
2. 50%.
3. Answers:

- a. The business owners failed to understand the market needs. They didn't perform a careful business plan before jumping into the market. Or they didn't stick to the original plan.
- b. The business owners failed to count the cost at the outset. They didn't have enough funding for the business, and they didn't realize the amount of time and money it would take to get this business off the ground. Or they just refused to commit the resources. (Jesus refers to this principle when speaking of the Christian life in Luke 14.)
- c. In some cases, the failed businesses were set up in a bad location. Or they failed to obtain adequate internet presence and effective marketing.
- d. In other cases, the business did not meet the market needs or expectations. To succeed in the restaurant business, for example, the start-up enterprise must excel at every point. The business must produce excellent food, offer the best service from a friendly, upbeat waiting staff, and maintain a

top-notch ambiance (decor, lighting, background music, etc.). Competition is stiff in this sector. The new business cannot afford to disappoint a single customer in the early years. New businesses cannot survive if attended by laziness and complacency. They must be adaptable to customer needs. If customers are asking for lemonade but all you have is iced tea to offer, you're on the road to failure. Both new businesses and older businesses must be adaptable to the ever-changing needs of their clientele.

- e. Going into debt and expanding too quickly is another failure point for new businesses. Be faithful in small things first. Before adding new products or new business departments, make sure you have the experience and the know-how to make it work.

4. Retired middle class/upper class older people would provide more business because they would have more money to spend.
5. Answers may vary.
6. 10, 1000.
7. Answers:
- a. $6,300 per week
- b. $1,536 per week
- c. $24,000 per month, or about $6,000 per week
8. The best way to assess market needs is to talk to people.
9. Examples include limited capital, government regulations, a bad location for your business, safety concerns for your employees, and limited access to resources.
10. You will need to take the time to develop your skills, learn from your mistakes, improve on your standards of quality, and earn a good reputation in the market. You will need to invest time and money into advertising to get your first customers.
11. It would be better to hire temporary employees or part-time employees.
12. Christian business owners should pay their employees before they pay themselves. In the situation that the business runs out of money for the payroll, the owner should draw from his or her own savings to pay the employees.
13. The Job Description.
14. Good managers are in constant communication with their workers, and most of it is going to be positive and encouraging. Also, they will provide an honest assessment of the work with a regular job performance review. Good managers are coaches.
15. The owners, the president, and the managers define the business culture.
16. The worst problem for businesses is employee turnover.
17. Ultimately, for Christians, the right business culture is hopefulness in the goodness of God. Love for God, reverence for God, love for others, gratitude for others, and honesty must form the pillars of a Christ-scented business culture.
18. Employees want to be:
- a. A Vital Part of the Team
- b. Successful and Appreciated.
- c. Trusted.

- d. Challenged
- e. Treated Fairly.

19. Is it true? Is it respectful? Is it necessary?
20. They will see themselves as serving their employees—bearing their burdens, helping with the tough projects, and exercising patient encouragement, coaching, and admonishing. They are willing to suffer more than the rest of the team, if necessary. Those who are gifted to lead and follow the example of Jesus will be good managers in businesses.

LIFE INTEGRATION AND SPIRITUAL APPLICATION

1. Answers may vary.
2. We will enter into the work week with an infectious enthusiasm, a joyful anticipation, and hopeful aspirations for what the week will bear out. We take it as a wonderful privilege to serve Christ.
3. Answers will vary.
4. Answers will vary.
5. Answers will vary.

CHAPTER 13

VOCABULARY AND TERMS

1. d
2. a
3. e
4. b
5. c

STUDY QUESTIONS

1. He has been drafted into the armed forces by the national government. A calling is a responsibility placed upon us from an outside source—a higher authority. God calls us to certain responsibilities in our lives too.
2. You can only achieve those goals which align with the will of God for your life.
3. God's calling for you is the specific responsibilities and work opportunities before you which best fit your talents, abilities, interests, and preparation (thus far in your life).
4. Your calling is more than your job, although it may include your job. Your calling includes your marriage if you are married. In this case, you are called to be a husband or a wife. Your calling includes the gifts you share in your local church body. Your calling includes raising children, fixing meals, changing diapers, providing hospitality, and discipling your own children.
5. If you are faced with three opportunities, choose the one that best fits your interests and abilities.
6. Secret (decretive) will. Revealed will. We can learn about His revealed will.
7. Righteousness, peace, and joy in the Holy Spirit. Peace speaks to your relationship with God and

with others. Joy comes in the presence of God, where the church meets together. Joy comes in the realization of God's salvation and the gospel of Christ (Hab. 3:17–18). Joy comes by answered prayer (John 16:24) and by reading God's Word (Ps. 119:111). Righteousness (in sanctification) comes by obeying God's Word.

8. Answers may vary.
9. Most young people should learn to type (ideally, at least 80 words per minute). Other important skills that come in handy today include speech and debate, graphic design, negotiating and selling, or basic household and auto repair.
10. Bootcamps, online tutorials, online college, and mentorships.
11. The college was a seminary for pastors. Later, liberal arts programs were put in place to present a humanist worldview, and to raise up more teachers to take that worldview into public schools.
12. The aggregate college student loan programs in the US have now topped $1.73 trillion (as of 2021). That's 8% of the GDP, up from 2.8% of the GDP in 2003.
13. Six years, as opposed to 9 months in 1975.
14. The best are nursing and engineering. The worst are drama, dance, zoology, visual arts, film, ecology, anthropology, fine arts, and music.
15. While only 25% of Swiss high school graduates take the college route, 70 percent opt for apprenticeship and early entry into the economy.

LIFE INTEGRATION AND SPIRITUAL APPLICATION

1. Answers will vary.
2. Answers will vary.
3. Answers:
- a. Dominion taker
- b. Provider for material needs of the home
- c. Defender and protector
- d. Sacrificial lover
- e. Shepherd and teacher of his children
- f. Answers will vary.
4. Answers:
- a. Helper for husband
- b. Home manager
- c. Modest (humble), generous, saved by childbearing
- d. Answers will vary.
5. Walk with wise men (and women).
6. Knowledge, spiritual accountability, and life integration.

FINAL EXAM

VOCABULARY AND TERMS

1. i
2. q
3. h
4. o
5. j
6. a
7. d
8. b
9. p
10. c
11. e
12. k
13. f
14. l
15. g
16. m
17. n

SHORT ANSWER

1. The Love of Money (Not money)
2. Mammon (or money)
3. Communism
4. Jubilee
5. Repay (or pay off the loans)
6. Reap

LONGER ANSWER

1. Knitting machine (weaver), Reaper, and Nail Gun.
2. Bad (tyrannical) governments
3. Price stability, scarcity, universal desirability, divisibility, portability, durability
4. Deceitful people would shave off small amounts of silver and gold from the coins. Or they would debase the money by mixing cheap metals into the coins.
5. A run on the bank occurs when a lot of depositors try to withdraw their money, but the banks don't hold enough money to provide for all the withdrawals.
6. The Federal Reserve System/Board.

7. B and C.
8. Death penalty
9. The confidence of the unbeliever is in himself (or man). The confidence of the believer is in God.
10. Joseph was very aware that God was watching him.

BASIC ACCOUNTING

1. The business earned $240 in profit.
2. $50. $40 lost by inflation.
3. $3030.
4. $200.
5. $550 billion.
6. He lost $20,000. He still owes the bank $10,000.
7. $2,800 annual income. $233.33.